Allyn and Bacon
Quick Guide to the Internet
for Composition

Allyn and Bacon

Quick Guide to the Internet for Composition

1999 Edition

H. Eric Branscomb

Salem State College

Doug Gotthoffer

California State University–Northridge

Allyn and Bacon

Boston • London • Toronto • Sydney • Tokyo • Singapore

Vice President and Director, Allyn and Bacon Interactive: Kevin B. Stone
Multimedia Editor: Marnie S. Greenhut
Editorial Production Administrator, Media: Robert Tonner
Cover Designer: Jennifer Hart
Editorial Production Service: Omegatype Typography, Inc.

NOTICE: Between the time web site information is gathered and then published it is not unusual for some sites to have closed. Also, the transcription of URLs can result in unintended typographical errors. The publisher would appreciate notification where these occcur so that they may be corrected in subsequent editions. Thank you.

TRADEMARK CREDITS: Where information was available, trademarks and registered trademarks are indicated below. When detailed information was not available, the publisher has indicated trademark status with an initial capital where those names appear in the text.

Macintosh is a registered trademark of Apple Computer, Inc.

Microsoft is a registered trademark of Microsoft Corporation. Windows, Windows95, and Microsoft Internet Explorer are trademarks of Microsoft Corporation.

Netscape and the Netscape Navigator logo are registered trademarks of Netscape Communications Corporation.

ISBN 2-205-29743-9

Printed in the United States of America

10   9   8   7   6   5   4   3   2   1   01   00   99   98

Contents

Part 1   Introduction to the Internet

Some Things You Ought to Know   1

A Brief History of the Internet   3

Using the World Wide Web for Research   4

In the Name of the Page   6

The URL Exposed   7

Getting There from Here   9

You Can Go Home (and to Other Pages) Again   11

Searching and Search Engines   11

Internet Gold Is Where You Find It   12

The (E)mail Goes Through   18

Welcome to the Internet, Miss Manners   21

Keeping Things to Yourself   22

A Discussion of Lists   24

And Now the News(group)   27

Welcome to the Internet, Miss Manners—Again   30

Give Your Web Browser Some Personality—Yours   31

The Information Explosion   32

Significance for Communication, Education, and Research   33

Open Topics   34

Writing about Literature   36

Publishing and Receiving Feedback on your Writing   37

Redline   38

Finding Help (OWLs)   40

Using the Internet for Research Papers   41

Online Library Resources   42

Special Cases   45

Writing for the Internet   45

Composing Web Pages   49

Final Words   50

Critical Evaluation   50

Part 2   Internet Activities for College Composition

    The Warmups   56

    The Hunt (WWW)   58

    A Closer Look at Hunting   64

    Beyond Search Engines   66

    More Composition Activities   67

    RESOURCES FOR INTERNET RESEARCH ON COMPOSITION   67

    Search Engines   67

    Fee-Based Research Services   69

    General Directories   70

    Desktop References   72

    Writing Help   73

    Writing for the Internet   79

    Evaluating Information on the Internet   80

    Specialized Web Sites   82

    Current Events   88

    Bibliographic Citation Guides   90

    FInding Email Addresses   91

    DOCUMENTATION   92

    MLA Documentation of Electronic Sources   92

    APA Documentation of Electronic Sources   110

Glossary   **115**

Allyn and Bacon
Quick Guide to the Internet
for Composition

Introduction
to the Internet

You're about to embark on an exciting experience as you become one of the millions of citizens of the Internet. In spite of what you might have heard, the Internet can be mastered by ordinary people before they earn a college degree and even if they're not majoring in rocket science.

Some Things You Ought to Know

Much of the confusion over the Internet comes from two sources. One is terminology. Just as the career you're preparing for has its own special vocabulary, so does the Internet. You'd be hard pressed to join in the shoptalk of archeologists, librarians, or carpenters if you didn't speak their language. Don't expect to plop yourself down in the middle of the Internet without some buzzwords under your belt, either.

The second source of confusion is that there are often many ways to accomplish the same ends on the Internet. This is a direct by-product of the freedom so highly cherished by Net citizens. When someone has an idea for doing something, he or she puts it out there and lets the Internet community decide its merits. As a result, it's difficult to put down in writing the *one exact* way to send email or find information on slugs or whatever.

Most of the material you'll encounter in this book applies to programs that run on the Macintosh computer. If you own or use a PC, you'll discover there are some cosmetic and technical differences. On the other hand, both computers offer the same major functionality. What you can

1

do on the Mac you can usually do on the PC, and vice versa. If you can't find a particular command or function mentioned in the book on your computer, chances are it's there, but in a different place or with a slightly different name. Check the manual or online help that came with your computer, or ask a more computer-savvy friend or professor.

And relax. Getting up to speed on the Internet takes a little time, but the effort will be well rewarded. Approach learning your way around the Internet with the same enthusiasm and curiosity you approach learning your way around a new college campus. This isn't a competition. Nobody's keeping score. And the only winner will be you.

In *Understanding Media,* Marshall McLuhan presaged the existence of the Internet when he described electronic media as an extension of our central nervous system. On the other hand, today's students introduced to the Internet for the first time describe it as "Way cool."

No matter which description you favor, you are immersed in a period in our culture that is transforming the way we live by transforming the nature of the information we live by. As recently as 1980, intelligence was marked by "knowing things." If you were born in that year, by the time you were old enough to cross the street by yourself, that definition had changed radically. Today, in a revolution that makes McLuhan's vision tangible, events, facts, rumors, and gossip are distributed instantly to all parts of the global body. The effects are equivalent to a shot of electronic adrenaline. No longer the domain of the privileged few, information is shared by all the inhabitants of McLuhan's global village. Meanwhile, the concept of information as intelligence feels as archaic as a television remote control with a wire on it (ask your parents about that).

With hardly more effort than it takes to rub your eyes open in the morning you can connect with the latest news, with gossip about your favorite music group or TV star, with the best places to eat on spring break, with the weather back home, or with the trials and tribulations of that soap opera character whose life conflicts with your history class.

You can not only carry on a real-time conversation with your best friend at a college half a continent away you can see and hear her, too. Or, you can play interactive games with a dozen or more world-wide, world-class, challengers; and that's just for fun.

When it comes to your education, the Internet has shifted the focus from amassing information to putting that information to use. Newspaper and magazine archives are now almost instantly available, as are the contents of many reference books. Distant and seemingly unapproachable, experts are found answering questions in discussion groups or in electronic newsletters.

The Internet also addresses the major problem facing all of us in our split-second, efficiency-rated culture: Where do we find the time? The

part

1

Internet allows professors and students to keep in touch, to collaborate and learn, without placing unreasonable demands on individual schedules. Professors are posting everything from course syllabi to homework solutions on the Internet, and are increasingly answering questions online, all in an effort to ease the pressure for face-to-face meetings by supplementing them with cyberspace offices. The Internet enables students and professors to expand office hours into a twenty-four-hour-a-day, seven-day-a-week operation. Many classes have individual sites at which enrolled students can gather electronically to swap theories, ideas, resources, gripes, and triumphs.

By freeing us from some of the more mundane operations of information gathering, and by sharpening our information-gathering skills in other areas, the Internet encourages us to be more creative and imaginative. Instead of devoting most of our time to gathering information and precious little to analyzing and synthesizing it, the Internet tips the balance in favor of the skills that separate us from silicon chips. Other Internet citizens can gain the same advantage, however, and as much as the Internet ties us together, it simultaneously emphasizes our individual skills—our ability to connect information in new, meaningful, and exciting ways. Rarely have we had the opportunity to make connections and observations on such a wide range of topics, to create more individual belief systems, and to chart a path through learning that makes information personally useful and meaningful.

part

1

A Brief History of the Internet

The 20th century's greatest advance in personal communication and freedom of expression began as a tool for national defense. In the mid-1960s, the Department of Defense was searching for an information analogy to the new Interstate Highway System, a way to move computations and computing resources around the country in the event the Cold War caught fire. The immediate predicament, however, had to do with the Defense Department's budget, and the millions of dollars spent on computer research at universities and think tanks. Much of these millions was spent on acquiring, building, or modifying large computer systems to meet the demands of the emerging fields of computer graphics, artificial intelligence, and multiprocessing (where one computer was shared among dozens of different tasks).

While this research was distributed across the country, the unwieldy, often temperamental, computers were not. Though researchers at MIT had spare time on their computer, short of packing up their notes and traveling to Massachusetts, researchers at Berkeley had no way to use it. Instead, Berkeley computer scientists would wind up duplicating MIT hardware in California. Wary of being accused of re-inventing the wheel, the Advanced Research Projects Agency (ARPA), the funding arm of the Defense Department, invested in the ARPANET, a private network that would allow disparate computer systems to communicate with each other. Researchers could remain ensconced among their colleagues at their home campuses while using computing resources at government research sites thousands of miles away.

A small cadre of ARPANET citizens soon began writing computer programs to perform little tasks across the Internet. Most of these programs, while ostensibly meeting immediate research needs, were written for the challenge of writing them. These programmers, for example, created the first email systems. They also created games like Space Wars and Adventure. Driven in large part by the novelty and practicality of email, businesses and institutions accepting government research funds begged and borrowed their way onto the ARPANET, and the number of connections swelled.

As the innocence of the 1960s gave way the business sense of the 1980s, the government eased out of the networking business, turning the ARPANET (now Internet) over to its users. While we capitalize the word "Internet", it may surprise you to learn there is no "Internet, Inc.," no business in charge of this uniquely postmodern creation. Administration of this world-wide communication complex is still handled by the cooperating institutions and regional networks that comprise the Internet. The word "Internet" denotes a specific interconnected network of networks, and not a corporate entity.

Using the World Wide Web for Research

Just as no one owns the worldwide communication complex that is the Internet, there is no formal organization among the collection of hundreds of thousands of computers that make up the part of the Net called the World Wide Web.

If you've never seriously used the Web, you are about to take your first steps on what can only be described as an incredible journey. Initially, though, you might find it convenient to think of the Web as a giant television network with millions of channels. It's safe to say that, among all these channels, there's something for you to watch. Only, how to find it? You could click through the channels one by one, of course, but by the time you found something of interest it would (1) be over or (2) leave you wondering if there wasn't something better on that you're missing.

A more efficient way to search for what you want would be to consult some sort of TV listing. While you could skim through pages more rapidly than channels, the task would still be daunting. A more creative approach would allow you to press a button on your remote control that would connect you to a channel of interest; what's more, that channel would contain the names (or numbers) of other channels with similar programs. Those channels in turn would contain information about other channels. Now you could zip through this million-channel universe, touching down only at programs of potential interest. This seems far more effective than the hunt-and-peck method of the traditional couch potato.

If you have a feel for how this might work for television, you have a feel for what it's like to journey around (or surf) the Web. Instead of channels on the Web, we have *Web sites*. Each site contains one or more *pages*. Each page may contain, among other things, links to other pages, either in the same site or in other sites, anywhere in the world. These other pages may elaborate on the information you're looking at or may direct you to related but not identical information, or even provide contrasting or contradictory points of view; and, of course, these pages could have links of their own.

Web sites are maintained by businesses, institutions, affinity groups, professional organizations, government departments, and ordinary people anxious to express opinions, share information, sell products, or provide services. Because these Web sites are stored electronically, updating them is more convenient and practical than updating printed media. That makes Web sites far more dynamic than other types of research material you may be used to, and it means a visit to a Web site can open up new opportunities that weren't available as recently as a few hours ago.

Hypertext and Links

The invention that unveils these revolutionary possibilities is called *hypertext*. Hypertext is a technology for combining text, graphics, sounds, video, and links on a single World Wide Web page. Click on a link and you're transported, like Alice falling down the rabbit hole, to a new page, a new address, a new environment for research and communication.

Links come in three flavors: text, picture, and hot spot. A text link may be a letter, a word, a phrase, a sentence, or any contiguous combination of text characters. You can identify text links at a glance because

Text Link

Picture Link

Text links are underlined and set off in color. Picture links are set off by a colored border. Hot spots carry no visual identification.

the characters are <u>underlined</u>, and are often displayed in a unique color, setting the link apart from the rest of the text on the page. Picture links are pictures or other graphic elements. On the Web, a picture may not only be worth a thousand words, but it may also be the start of a journey into a whole new corner of cyberspace.

The third kind of link, the hot spot, is neither underlined nor bordered, a combination which would make it impossible to spot, were it not for a Web convention that offers you a helping hand finding all types of links. This helping hand is, well, a hand. Whenever the mouse cursor passes over a link, the cursor changes from an arrow to a hand. Wherever you see the hand icon, you can click and retrieve another Web page. Sweep the cursor over an area of interest, see the hand, follow the link, and you're surfing the Web.

In the Name of the Page

Zipping around the Web in this way may seem exciting, even serendipitous, but it's also fraught with perils. How, for instance, do you revisit a page of particular interest? Or share a page with a classmate? Or cite a page as a reference for a professor? Web page designers assign names, or titles, to their pages; unfortunately, there's nothing to prevent two designers from assigning the same title to different pages.

An instrument that uniquely identifies Web pages does exist. It's called a Universal Resource Locator (URL), the cyber-signposts of the World Wide Web. URLs contain all the information necessary to locate:

- the page containing the information you're looking for;
- the computer that hosts (stores) that page of information;
- the form the information is stored in.

A typical URL looks like this:

```
http://www.abacon.com/homepage.html
```

You enter it into the **Location** field at the top of your browser window. Hit the **Return** (or **Enter**) key and your browser will deliver to your screen the exact page specified. When you click on a link, you're actually using a shorthand alternative to typing the URL yourself because the browser does it for you. In fact, if you watch the "Location" field when you click on a link, you'll see its contents change to the URL you're traveling to.

part

1

The URL Exposed

How does your browser—or the whole World Wide Web structure, for that matter—know where you're going? As arcane as the URL appears, there is a logical explanation to its apparent madness. (This is true not only of URLs but also of your computer experience in general. Because a computer's "intelligence" only extends to following simple instructions exactly, most of the commands, instructions, and procedures you'll encounter have simple underlying patterns. Once you familiarize yourself with these patterns, you'll find you're able to make major leaps in your understanding of new Internet features.)

To unscramble the mysteries of World Wide Web addresses, we'll start at the end of the URL and work our way toward the front.

```
/homepage.html
```

This is the name of a single file or document. Eventually, the contents of this file/document will be transferred over the Internet to your computer.

However, because there are undoubtedly thousands of files on the Internet with this name, we need to clarify our intentions a bit more.

```
www.abacon.com
```

This is the name of a particular Internet *Web server,* a computer whose job it is to forward Web pages to you on request. By Internet convention, this name is unique. The combination of

```
www.abacon.com/homepage.html
```

identifies a unique file/document on a unique Web server on the World Wide Web. No other file has this combined address, so there's no question about which file/document to transfer to you.

The characters *http://* at the beginning of the URL identify the method by which the file/document will be transferred. The letters stand for HyperText Transfer Protocol.

part

1

Quick Check

Don't Be Lost In (Hyper)Space

Let's pause for a quick check of your Web navigation skills. Look at the sample web page on the next page. How many links does it contain?

Did you find all five? That's right, five:

- The word "links" in the second line below the seaside picture;
- The sentence "What about me?";
- The word "cyberspace" in the quick brown fox sentence;
- The red and white graphic in the lower left-hand corner of the page. The blue border around it matches the blue of the text links;
- The hot spot in the seaside picture. We know there's at least one link in the picture, because the cursor appears as a hand. (There may be more hot spots on the page, but we can't tell from this picture alone.)

A sample web page to exercise your link identifying skills.

Getting There from Here

Now you know that a URL uniquely identifies a page and that links used as shorthand for URLs enable you to travel from page to page in the Web; but what if a link takes you someplace you don't want to go? Missing page messages take several forms, such as URL 404, Object not on this server, Missing Object, Page not Found, but they all lead to the same place—a dead end. The page specified by the link or URL no longer exists. There are many reasons for missing pages. You may have entered the URL incorrectly. Every character must be precise and no spaces are allowed. More than likely, though, especially if you arrived here via a link, the page you're after has been moved or removed. Remember, anybody can create a link to any page. In the spirit of the Internet, there are no forms to fill out, no procedures to follow. That's the

part

1

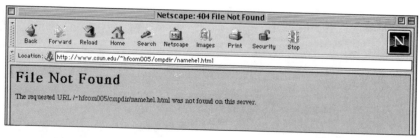

A missing page message, an all too common road hazard on the information superhighway.

good news. The bad news is that the owner of a page is under no obligation to inform the owners of links pointing to it that the page location has changed. In fact, there's no way for the page owner to even know about all the links to her page. Yes, the Internet's spirit of independence proves frustrating sometimes, but you'll find these small inconveniences are a cheap price to pay for the benefits you receive. Philosophy aside, though, we're still stuck on a page of no interest to us. The best strategy is to back up and try another approach.

Every time you click on the **Back** button, you return to the previous page you visited. That's because your browser keeps track of the pages you visit and the order in which you visit them. The **Back** icon, and its counterpart, the **Forward** icon, allow you to retrace the steps, forward and backward, of your cyberpath. Sometimes you may want to move two, three, or a dozen pages at once. Although you can click the **Back** or **Forward** icons multiple times, Web browsers offer an easier navigation shortcut. Clicking on the **Go** menu in the menu bar displays a list of your most recently visited pages, in the order you've been there. Unlike the **Back** or **Forward** icons, you can select any page from the menu, and a single click takes you directly there. There's no need to laboriously move one page at a time.

Quick Check

As a quick review, here's what we know about navigating the Web so far:

■ Enter a URL directly into the Location field;
■ Click on a link;
■ Use the **Back** or **Forward** icons;
■ Select a page from the **Go** menu.

You Can Go Home (and to Other Pages) Again

How do we return to a page hours, days, or even months later? One way is to write down the URLs of every page we may want to revisit. There's got to be a better way, and there is: We call them bookmarks (on Netscape Communicator) or favorites (on Microsoft Internet Explorer).

Like their print book namesakes, Web bookmarks (and favorites) flag specific Web pages. Selecting an item from the **Bookmark/Favorites** menu, like selecting an item from the **Go** menu, is the equivalent of entering a URL into the **Location** field of your browser, except that items in the **Bookmark/Favorites** menu are ones you've added yourself and represent pages visited over many surfing experiences, not just the most recent one.

To select a page from your bookmark list, pull down the **Bookmark/Favorites** menu and click on the desired entry. In Netscape Communicator, clicking on the **Add Bookmark** command makes a bookmark entry for the current page. **Add Page to Favorites** performs the same function in Microsoft Internet Explorer.

To save a favorite page location, use the **Add** feature available on both browsers. Clicking that feature adds the location of the current page to your **Bookmark/Favorites** menu. A cautionary note is in order here. Your bookmark or favorites list physically exists only on your personal computer, which means that if you connect to the Internet on a different computer, your list won't be available. If you routinely connect to the Internet from a computer lab, for example, get ready to carry the URLs for your favorite Web sites in your notebook or your head.

part

1

Searching and Search Engines

Returning to our cable television analogy, you may recall that we conveniently glossed over the question of how we selected a starting channel in the first place. With a million TV channels, or several million Web pages, we can't depend solely on luck guiding us to something interesting.

On the Web, we solve the problem with specialized computer programs called *search engines* that crawl through the Web, page by page, cataloging its contents. As different software designers developed search strategies, entrepreneurs established Web sites where any user could find pages containing particular words and phrases. Today, Web sites such as Yahoo!, AltaVista, Excite, WebCrawler, and MetaCrawler offer you a "front door" to the Internet that begins with a search for content of interest.

The URLs for some popular search sites are:

Excite	www.excite.com
Yahoo!	www.yahoo.com
AltaVista	www.altavista.digital.com
WebCrawler	www.webcrawler.com
MetaCrawler	www.metacrawler.com
Infoseek	www.infoseek.com
EBlast	www.eblast.com
HotBot	www.hotbot.com

Internet Gold Is Where You Find It

Let's perform a simple search using HotBot to find information about the history of the Internet.

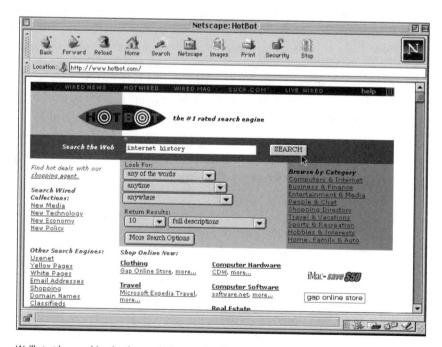

We'll start by searching for the words "internet" or "history." By looking for "any of the words," the search will return pages on which either "internet" or "history" or both appear.

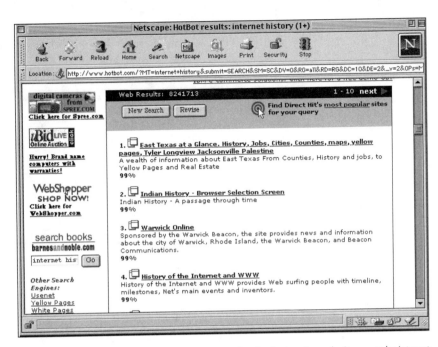

Our search returned 12,334,156 matches or *hits*. Note that the first two items don't seem to be Internet history–related. The percentage number in the last line of each summary indicates the "quality" of the match, usually related to the number of times the search word(s) appears on the page.

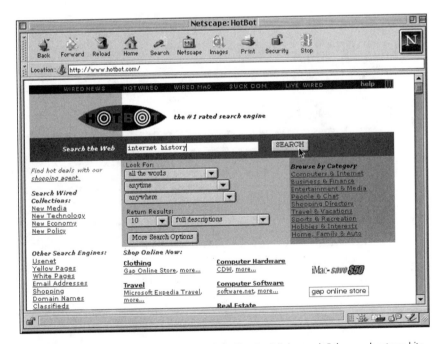

When we conduct the same search, but this time looking for "all the words," the search returns hits when both "internet" and "history" appear on the same page, in any order, and not necessarily next to each other.

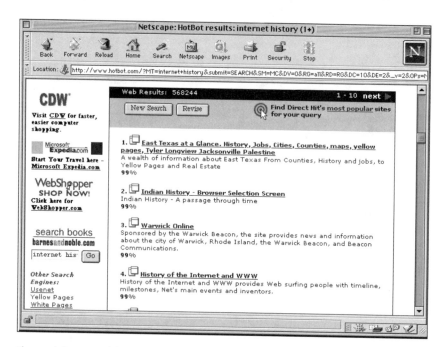

The search is narrowed down to only 885,911 hits. Note that the first four items are the same as in the previous search.

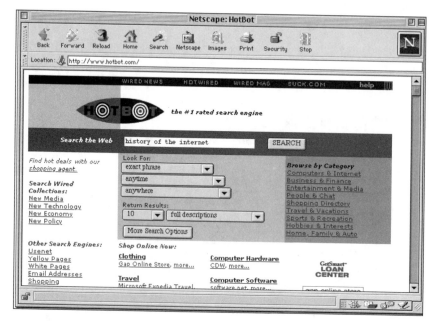

When we search for the exact phrase "history of the internet," which means those four words in exactly that order, with no intervening words, we're down to less than 12,000 hits (still a substantial number). This time, the first two hits look dead-on, and the third is a possibility, if we knew what "GTO" meant. The fourth hit is strange, so we click on it to check it out.

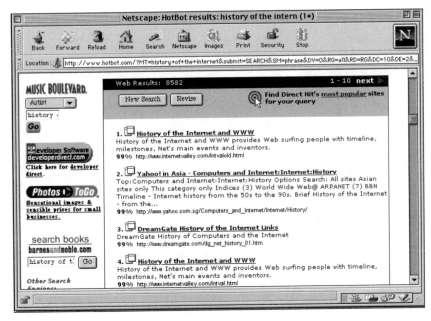

This hit seems to have nothing to do with the history of the Internet. Hits happen. No search engine is 100 percent accurate 100 percent of the time. Spurious search results are the serendipity of the Internet. Look at them as an opportunity to explore something new.

part

1

Out of curiosity, let's try our history of the Internet search using a different search engine. When we search for the phrase "history of the internet" using WebCrawler, the quotation marks serve the same purpose as selecting "the exact phrase" option in Hotbot. The WebCrawler search only finds 504 hits. Some are the same as those found using HotBot, some are different. Different searching strategies and software algorithms make using more than one search engine a must for serious researchers.

The major search engines conveniently provide you with tips to help you get the most out of their searches. These include ways to use AND and OR to narrow down searches, and ways to use NOT to eliminate unwanted hits.

Each search engine also uses a slightly different approach to cataloging the Web, so at different sites your results might vary. Often, one search engine provides better results (more relevant hits) in your areas of interest; sometimes, the wise strategy is to provide the same input to several different engines. No one search engine does a perfect job all the time, so experience will dictate the one that's most valuable for you.

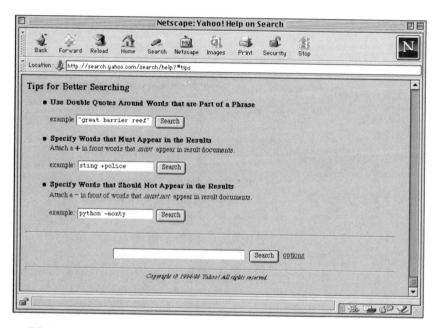

You'll find search tip pages like this at all the major searcch engine sites.

Quick Check

Let's review our searching strategies:

- Visit one of the search engine sites;
- Enter key words or phrases that best describe the search criteria;
- Narrow the search if necessary by using options such as "all the words" or "the exact phrase." On some search engines, you may use the word "and" or the symbol "|" to indicate words that all must appear on a page;
- Try using the same criteria with different search engines.

How Not to Come Down with a Virus

Downloading files from the Internet allows less responsible Net citizens to unleash onto your computer viruses, worms, and Trojan horses, all dangerous programs that fool you into thinking they're doing one thing while they're actually erasing your hard disk or performing some other undesirable task. Protection is your responsibility.

One way to reduce the risk of contracting a virus is to download software from reliable sites. Corporations such as Microsoft and Apple take care to make sure downloadable software is virus free. So do most institutions that provide software downloads as a public service (such as the Stanford University archives of Macintosh software). Be especially careful of programs you find on someone's home page. If you're not sure about safe download sources, ask around in a newsgroup (discussed shortly), talk to friends, or check with the information technology center on campus.

You can also buy and use a reliable virus program. Norton, Symantec, and Dr. Solomon all sell first-rate programs for the Mac and PC. You can update these programs right from the Internet so they'll detect the most current viruses. Most of the time, these programs can disinfect files/documents on your disk that contain viruses. Crude as it may sound, downloading programs from the Internet without using a virus check is like having unprotected sex with a stranger. While downloading software may not be life threatening, imagine the consequences if your entire hard disk, including all your course work and software, is totally obliterated. It won't leave you feeling very good.

part

1

If you'd like some entertaining practice sharpening your Web searching skills, point your browser to <www.internettreasurehunt.com>, follow the directions, and you're on your way to becoming an Internet researcher extraordinaire.

The (E)mail Goes Through

Email was one of the first applications created for the Internet by its designers, who sought a method of communicating with each other directly from their keyboards. Your electronic Internet mailbox is to email what a post office box is to "snail mail" (the name Net citizens apply to ordinary, hand-delivered mail). This mailbox resides on the computer of your Internet Service Provider (ISP). That's the organization providing you with your Internet account. Most of the time your ISP will be your school; but, you may contract with one of the commercial providers, such as America Online, Netcom, Microsoft Network, Earthlink, or AT&T. The Internet doesn't deliver a message to your door but instead leaves it in a conveniently accessible place (your mailbox) in the post office (the computer of your ISP), until you retrieve the mail using your combination (password).

If you currently have computer access to the Internet, your school or ISP assigned you a *user name* (also called a user id, account name, or account number). This user name may be your first name, your first initial and the first few characters of your last name, or some strange combination of numbers and letters only a computer could love. An email address is a combination of your user name and the unique address of the computer through which you access your email, like this:

```
username@computername.edu
```

The three letters after the dot, in this case "edu," identify the top level "domain." There are six common domain categories in use: edu (educational), com (commercial), org (organization), net (network), mil (military), and gov (government). The symbol "@"—called the "at" sign in typewriter days—serves two purposes: For computers, it provides a neat, clean separation between your user name and the computer name; for people, it makes Internet addresses more pronounceable. Your address is read: user name "at" computer name "dot" e-d-u. Suppose your Internet user name is "a4736g" and your ISP is Allyn & Bacon, the publisher of this book. Your email address might look like

```
a4736g@abacon.com
```

and you would tell people your email address is "ay-four-seven-three-six-gee at ay bacon dot com."

We Don't Just Handle Your Email, We're Also a Client

You use email with the aid of special programs called *mail clients*. As with search engines, mail clients have the same set of core features, but your access to these features varies with the type of program. On both the PC and the Mac, Netscape Communicator and Microsoft Internet Explorer give you access to mail clients while you're plugged into the Web. That way you can pick up and send mail while you're surfing the Web.

The basic email service functions are creating and sending mail, reading mail, replying to mail, and forwarding mail. First we'll examine the process of sending and reading mail, and then we'll discuss how to set up your programs so that your messages arrive safely.

Let's look at a typical mail client screen, in this case from Netscape Communicator 4. You reach this screen by choosing **Messenger Inbox** from the menu. Along the top of the screen are icons denoting the basic mail service functions. To send a message from scratch, choose the **New Msg** icon to create a blank message form, which has fields for the recipient's address and the subject, and a window for the text of the message.

Fill in the recipient's address in the "To" field, just above the arrow. Use your own address. We'll send email to ourselves and use the same

part

1

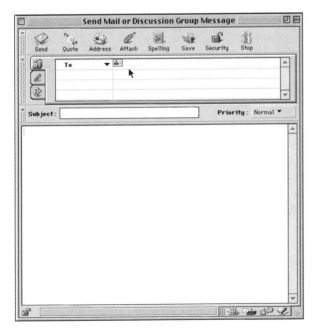

New message form, with fields for recipient's address and the subject, and a window for the text of the message.

message to practice sending email and reading it as well; then we'll know if your messages come out as expected.

Click in the "Subject" field and enter a word or phrase that generally describes the topic of the message. Since we're doing this for the first time, let's type "Maiden Email Voyage."

Now click anywhere in the text window and enter your message. Let's say "Hi. Thanks for guiding me through sending my first email." You'll find that the mail client works here like a word processing program, which means you can insert and delete words and characters and highlight text.

Now click the **Send** icon. You've just created and sent your first email message. In most systems, it takes a few seconds to a few minutes for a message to yourself to reach your mailbox, so you might want to take a short break before continuing. When you're ready to proceed, close the **Send Mail** window and click the **Get Msg** icon in the **Inbox** window.

What Goes Around Comes Around

Now let's grab hold of the message you just sent to yourself. When retrieving mail, most mail clients display a window showing the messages in your mailbox telling you how many new messages have been added.

If you've never used your email before, chances are your message window is empty, or contains only one or two messages (usually official messages from the ISP) besides the one you sent to yourself. The message to yourself should be accompanied by an indicator of some sort—a colored mark, the letter N—indicating it's a new message. In Netscape Communicator, as in other mail clients, you also get to see the date of the message, who sent it, and the information you entered in the subject line. The Subject field lets you scan your messages and determine which ones you want to look at first.

The summary of received messages tells you everything you need to know about a message except what's in it. Click anywhere in the line to see the contents in the message window. Click on the message from yourself and you'll see the contents of the message displayed in a window. The information at the top—To, From, Subject, and so forth—is called the *header*. Depending on your system, you may also see some cryptic lines with terms such as X-Mailer, received by, and id number. Most of the time, there's nothing in this part of the header of interest, so just skip over it for now.

Moving Forward

The contents, or text, of your message can be cut and pasted just like any other text document. If you and a classmate are working on a project together, your partner can write part of a paper and email it to you, and you can copy the text from your email message and paste it into your word processing program.

What if there are three partners in this project? One partner sends you a draft of the paper for you to review. You like it and want to send it on to your other partner. The **Forward** feature lets you send the message intact, so you don't have to cut and paste it into a new message window. To forward a message, highlight it in the **Inbox** (top) and click the **Forward** icon. Enter the recipient's address in the "To" field of the message window. Note that the subject of the message is "Fwd:" followed by the subject of the original message. Use the text window to add your comments ahead of the original message.

A Chance to Reply

Email is not a one-way message system. Let's walk through a reply to a message from a correspondent named Elliot. Highlight the message in your **Inbox** again and this time click on the **Reply** icon. When the message window appears, click on the **Quote** icon. Depending on which program you're using, you'll see that each line in the message is preceded by either a vertical bar or a right angle bracket (>).

Note the vertical line to the left of the original text. The "To" and "Subject" fields are filled in automatically with the address of the sender and the original subject preceded by "Re:". In Internet terminology, the message has been *quoted*. The vertical bar or > is used to indicate lines not written by you but by someone else (in this case, the message's original author). Why bother? Because this feature allows you to reply without retyping the parts of the message you're responding to. Because your typing isn't quoted, your answers stand out from the original message. Netscape Communicator 4 adds some blank lines above and below your comments, a good practice for you if your mail client doesn't do this automatically.

Welcome to the Internet, Miss Manners

While we're on the subject of email, here are some *netiquette* (net etiquette) tips.

- When you send email to someone, even someone who knows you well, all they have to look at are your words—there's no body language attached. That means there's no smile, no twinkle in the eye, no raised eyebrow; and especially, there's no tone of voice. What you write is open to interpretation and your recipient has nothing to guide him or her. You may understand the context of a remark, but will your reader? If you have any doubts about how your message will be interpreted, you might want to tack on an *emoticon* to your message. An emoticon is a face created out of keyboard characters. For example, there's the happy Smiley :-) (you have to look at it sideways . . . the parenthesis is its mouth), the frowning Smiley :-((Frownie?), the winking Smiley ;-), and so forth. Smileys are the body language of the Internet. Use them to put remarks in context. "Great," in response to a friend's suggestion means you like the idea. "Great :-(" changes the meaning to one of disappointment or sarcasm. (Want a complete list of emoticons? Try using "emoticon" as a key word for a Web search.)

part

1

- Keep email messages on target. One of the benefits of email is its speed. Reading through lengthy messages leaves the reader wondering when you'll get to the point.

- Email's speed carries with it a certain responsibility. Its ease of use and the way a messages seems to cry out for an answer both encourage quick responses, but quick doesn't necessarily mean thoughtful. Once you hit the **Send** icon, that message is gone. There's no recall button. Think before you write, lest you feel the wrath of the modern-day version of your parents' adage: Answer in haste, repent at leisure.

Keeping Things to Yourself

Here's another tip cum cautionary note, this one about Web security. Just as you take care to protect your wallet or purse while walking down a crowded street, it's only good practice to exercise caution with information you'd like to keep (relatively) private. Information you pass around the Internet is stored on, or passed along by, computers that are accessible to others. Although computer system administrators take great care to insure the security of this information, no scheme is completely infallible. Here are some security tips:

- Exercise care when sending sensitive information such as credit card numbers, passwords, even telephone numbers and addresses in plain email. Your email message may pass through four or five computers en route to its destination, and at any of these points, it can be intercepted and read by someone other than the recipient.

- Send personal information over the Web only if the page is secure. Web browsers automatically encrypt information on secure pages, and the information can only be unscrambled at the Web site that created the secure page. You can tell if a page is secure by checking the status bar at the bottom of your browser's window for an icon of a closed lock.

- Remember that any files you store on your ISP's computer are accessible to unscrupulous hackers.

- Protect your password. Many Web client programs, such as mail clients, have your password for you. That means anyone with physical access to your computer can read your email. With a few simple tools, someone can even steal your password. Never leave your password on a lab computer. (Make sure the **Remember Password** or **Save Password** box is unchecked in any application that asks for your password.)

part

1

The closed lock icon in the lower left-hand corner of your browser window indicates a "secure" Web page.

An Audience Far Wider Than You Imagine

Remember that the Web in particular and the Internet in general are communications mediums with a far-reaching audience, and placing information on the Internet is tantamount to publishing it. Certainly, the contents of any message or page you post become public information, but in a newsgroup (an electronic bulletin board), your email address also becomes public knowledge. On a Web page, posting a photo of your favorite music group can violate the photographer's copyright, just as if you published the image in a magazine. Use common sense about posting information you or someone else expects to remain private; and, remember, information on the Web can and will be read by people with different tastes and sensitivities. The Web tends to be self-censoring, so be prepared to handle feedback, both good and bad.

A Discussion of Lists

There's no reason you can't use email to create a discussion group. You pose a question, for example, by sending an email message to everyone in the group. Somebody answers and sends the answer to everyone else on the list, and so on.

At least, that's the theory.

In practice, this is what often happens. As people join and leave the group, you and the rest of your group are consumed with updating your lists, adding new names and deleting old ones. As new people join, their addresses may not make it onto the lists of all the members of the group, so different participants get different messages. The work of administering the lists becomes worse than any value anyone can get out of the group, and so it quickly dissolves.

Generally, you're better off letting the computer handle discussion group administration. A *list server* is a program for administering emailing lists. It automatically adds and deletes list members and handles the distribution of messages.

part

1

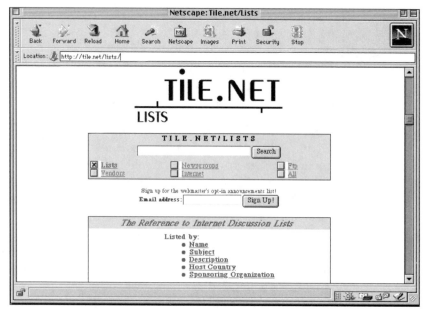

Tile.Net offfers shortcuts to working your way through the Internet's maze of discussion lists.

Thousands of mailing lists have already been formed by users with common interests. You may find mailing lists for celebrities, organizations, political interests, occupations, and hobbies. Your instructor may establish a mailing list for your course.

Groups come in several different flavors. Some are extremely active. You can receive as many as forty or more email messages a day. Other lists may send you a message a month. One-way lists, such as printed newsletters, do not distribute your reply to any other subscriber. Some lists distribute replies to everyone. These lists include mediated lists, in which an "editor" reviews each reply for suitability (relevance, tone, use of language) before distributing the message, and unmediated lists, in which each subscriber's response is automatically distributed to all the other subscribers with no restrictions except those dictated by decency and common sense, though these qualities may not always be obvious from reading the messages.

Get on a List Online

You join in the discussion by subscribing to a list, which is as straightforward as sending email. You need to know only two items: the name of the list and the address of the list server program handling subscriptions. To join a list, send a **Subscribe** message to the list server address. The message must contain the letters "Sub," the name of the list, and your name (your real name, not your user name), all on one line. *And that's all.* This message will be read by a computer program that looks for these items only. At the very best, other comments in the message will be ignored. At the very worst, your entire message will be ignored, and so will you.

Within a few hours to a day after subscribing, the list server will automatically send you a confirmation email message, including instructions for sending messages, finding out information about the list and its members, and canceling your subscription. Save this message for future reference. That way, if you do decide to leave the list, you won't have to circulate a message to the members asking how to unsubscribe, and you won't have to wade through fifty replies all relaying the same information you received when you joined.

Soon after your confirmation message appears in your mailbox, and depending on the activity level of the list, you'll begin receiving email messages. New list subscribers customarily wait a while before joining the discussion. After all, you're electronically strolling into a room full of strangers; it's only fair to see what topics are being discussed before

part

1

wading in with your own opinions. Otherwise, you're like the bore at the party who elbows his way into a conversation with "But enough about you, let's talk about me." You'll also want to avoid the faux pas of posting a long missive on a topic that subscribers spent the preceding three weeks thrashing out. Observe the list for a while, understand its tone and feel, what topics are of interest to others and what areas are taboo. Also, look for personalities. Who's the most vociferous? Who writes very little but responds thoughtfully? Who's the most flexible? The most rigid? Most of all, keep in mind that there are far more observers than participants. What you write may be read by 10 or 100 times more people than those whose names show up in the daily messages.

When you reply to a message, you reply to the list server address, not to the address of the sender (unless you intend for your communication to remain private). The list server program takes care of distributing your message listwide. Use the address in the "Reply To" field of the message. Most mail clients automatically use this address when you select the **Reply** command. Some may ask if you want to use the reply address (say yes). Some lists will send a copy of your reply to you so you know your message is online. Others don't send the author a copy, relying on your faith in the infallibility of computers.

In the words of those famous late night television commercials, you can cancel your subscription at any time. Simply send a message to the address you used to subscribe (which you'll find on that confirmation message you saved for reference), with "Unsub," followed on the same line by the name of the list. For example, to leave a list named "WRITER-L," you would send:

```
Unsub WRITER-L
```

Even if you receive messages for a short while afterwards, have faith—they will disappear.

Waste Not, Want Not

List servers create an excellent forum for people with common interests to share their views; however, from the Internet standpoint, these lists are terribly wasteful. First of all, if there are one thousand subscribers to a list, every message must be copied one thousand times and distributed over the Internet. If there are forty replies a day, this one list creates forty thousand email messages. Ten such lists mean almost a half million messages, most of which are identical, flying around the Net.

part

1

Another wasteful aspect of list servers is the way in which messages are answered. The messages in your mailbox on any given day represent a combination of new topics and responses to previous messages. But where are these previous messages? If you saved them, they're in your email mailbox taking up disk space. If you haven't saved them, you have nothing to compare the response to. What if a particular message touches off a chain of responses, with subscribers referring not only to the source message but to responses as well? It sounds like the only safe strategy is to save every message from the list, a suggestion as absurd as it is impractical.

What we really need is something closer to a bulletin board than a mailing list. On a bulletin board, messages are posted once. Similar notices wind up clustered together. Everyone comes to the same place to read or post messages.

And Now the News(group)

The Internet equivalent of the bulletin board is the Usenet or newsgroup area. Usenet messages are copied only once for each ISP supporting the newsgroup. If there are one thousand students on your campus reading the same newsgroup message, there need only be one copy of the message stored on your school's computer.

Categorizing a World of Information

Newsgroups are categorized by topics, with topics broken down into subtopics and sub-subtopics. For example, you'll find newsgroups devoted to computers, hobbies, science, social issues, and "alternatives." Newsgroups in this last category cover a wide range of topics that may not appeal to the mainstream. Also in this category are beginning newsgroups.

Usenet names are amalgams of their topics and subtopics, separated by dots. If you were interested in a newsgroup dealing with, say, music, you might start with rec.music and move down to rec.music.radiohead, or rec.music.techno, and so forth. The naming scheme allows you to zero in on a topic of interest.

Getting into the News(group) Business

Most of the work of reading, responding to, and posting messages is handled by a news reader client program, accessible through both Netscape Communicator and Microsoft Internet Explorer. You can not only surf the Web and handle your mail via your browser, but you can also drop into your favorite newsgroups virtually all in one operation.

Let's drop into a newsgroup. To reach groups via Netscape Communicator, select the **Message Center** icon, then select "news" from the message center window. Your news reader displays a list of available groups. In Netscape Communicator, this list appears in outline form to save space. Click on the arrows next to the folder names to move down the outline (through the categories) to see more groups.

To subscribe to a newsgroup—that is, to tell your news reader you want to be kept up-to-date on the messages posted to a particular group—highlight the group of interest and click on **Subscribe.** Alternately, you can click in the Subscribe column to the right of the group name. The check mark in the Subscribe column means you're "in."

part

1

The message center in Netscape Communicator displays a list of newsgroups on your subscription list. Double click on the one of current interest and your reader presents you with a list of messages posted on the group's bulletin board. Double click on a message to open its contents in a window.

Often, messages contain "Re:" in their subject lines, indicating a response to a previous message (the letters stand for "Regarding"). Many news readers maintain a *thread* for you. Threads are chains of messages and all responses to that message. These readers give you the option to read messages chronologically or to read a message followed by its responses.

When you subscribe to a newsgroup, your news reader will also keep track of the messages you've read so that it can present you with the newest (unread) ones. While older messages are still available to you, this feature guarantees that you stay up-to-date without any record keeping on your part. Subscribing to a newsgroup is free, and the subscription information resides on your computer.

Newsgroups have no way of knowing who their subscribers are, and the same caveat that applies to bookmarks applies to newsgroups. Information about your subscriptions resides physically on the personal computer you're using. If you switch computers, as in a lab, your subscription information and history of read messages are beyond your reach.

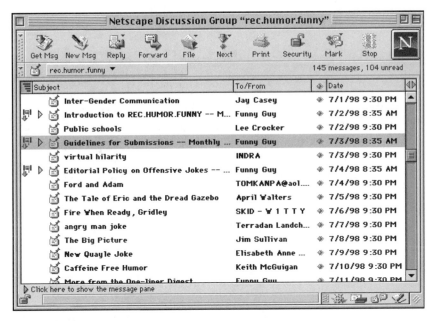

A listing of posted messages. While not visible from this black and white reproduction, a red indicator in the Subject column marks unread messages.

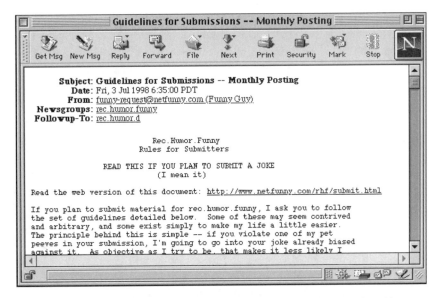

Double-clicking on a message opens its contents into a window like this. You can reply to this message via the Reply icon, or get the next message using the Next icon.

Welcome to the Internet, Miss Manners—Again

As with list servers, hang out for a while, or *lurk*, to familiarize yourself with the style, tone, and content of newsgroup messages. As you probably surmised from the names of the groups, their topics of discussion are quite narrow. One of the no-nos of newsgroups is posting messages on subjects outside the focus of the group. Posting off-topic messages, especially lengthy ones, is an excellent way to attract a flaming.

A *flame* is a brutally debasing message from one user to another. Flames are designed to hurt and offend, and often the target of the flame feels compelled to respond in kind to protect his or her self-esteem. This leads to a *flame war*, as other users take sides and wade in with flames of their own. If you find yourself the target of a flame, your best strategy is to ignore it. As with a campfire, if no one tends to the flames, they soon die out.

As mentioned earlier, posting messages to newsgroups is a modern form of publishing, and a publisher assumes certain responsibilities. You have a duty to keep your messages short and to the point. Many newsgroup visitors connect to the Internet via modems. Downloading a day's worth of long postings, especially uninteresting ones, is annoying and frustrating. Similarly, don't post the same message to multiple, related newsgroups. This is called *cross posting*, and it's a peeve of Net citizens who check into these groups. If you've ever flipped the television from channel to channel during a commercial break only to encounter the same commercial (an advertising practice called *roadblocking*), you can imagine how annoying it is to drop in on several newsgroups only to find the same messages posted to each one.

With the huge potential audience newsgroups offer, you might think you've found an excellent medium for advertising goods or services. After all, posting a few messages appears analogous to running classified ads in newspapers, only here the cost is free. There's a name for these kinds of messages—*spam*. Spam is the junk mail of the Internet, and the practice of spamming is a surefire way to attract flames. The best advice for handling spam? Don't answer it. Not only does an answer encourage the spammer, but he or she will also undoubtedly put your email address on a list and sell it to other spammers, who will flood your online mailbox with their junk.

Above all, be considerate of others. Treat them the way you'd like to be treated. Do you enjoy having your grammar or word choices corrected in front of the whole world? Do you feel comfortable when someone calls you stupid in public? Do you appreciate having your religion, ethnicity, heritage, or gender belittled in front of an audience? Respect the rights and feelings of others, if not out of simple decency then out of the sanctions your ISP may impose. Although you have every right to express an unpopular opinion or to take issue with the postings of others, most ISPs have regulations about the kinds of messages one can send via their facilities. Obscenities, threats, and spam may, at a minimum, result in your losing your Internet access privileges.

Give Your Web Browser Some Personality—Yours

Before accessing email and newsgroup functions, you need to set up or personalize your browser. If you always work on the same personal computer, this is a one-time operation that takes only a few minutes. In it, you tell your browser where to find essential computer servers, along with personal information the Internet needs to move messages for you.

part

1

- *Step 1:* Open the **Preferences** menu. In Netscape Communicator, it's located under the **Edit** menu; in Microsoft Internet Explorer, it's among the icons at the top of the screen.

- *Step 2:* Tell the browser who you are and where to find your mail servers. Your Reply To address is typically the same as your email address, though if you have an email alias you can use it here. Microsoft Internet Explorer has slots for your mail servers in the same window. Your ISP will provide the server names and addresses. Be sure to use your user name (and not your alias) in the "Account Name" field. SMTP handles your outgoing messages, while the POP3 server routes incoming mail. Often, but not always, these server names are the same. Netscape Communicator has a separate window for server names.

- *Step 3:* Tell the browser where to find your news server. Your ISP will furnish the name of the server. Note that in Microsoft Internet Explorer, you specify a helper application to read the news. Now that most computers come with browsers already loaded onto the hard disk, you'll find that these helper applications are already set up for you.

- *Step 4:* Set your home page. For convenience, you may want your browser to start by fetching a particular page, such as your favorite search site. Or you might want to begin at your school library's home page. Enter the URL for this starting page in the home page address field. Both Netscape and Microsoft offer the option of no home page when you start up. In that case, you get a blank browser window.

Operating systems such as Mac OS 8 and Microsoft Windows 95 offer automated help in setting up your browsers for Web, mail, and newsgroup operation. You need to know the names of the servers mentioned above, along with your user name and other details, such as the address of the domain name server (DNS) of your ISP. You should receive all this information when you open your Internet account. If not, ask for it.

The Information Explosion

The Internet has been a boon to college students, and nowhere will this be more evident than in your composition classes. Thanks to computer network technology, the day is fast approaching when you may be able to do all your research without leaving your room; write and submit your papers without using any paper; ask your teacher a question when he or she is a thousand miles away; and engage in conversations with other students or experts in a field when you're alone. That day hasn't arrived yet, but many of yesterday's dreams are realities today.

The Internet has intensified and accelerated the production and dissemination of information—in computerese, the input, output, and throughput have increased dramatically. There is exponentially more information and misinformation available; it's available more quickly and easily than ever before in the history of humankind. But the rules of dealing with this information have changed. Twenty years ago a major task of a student writing a research paper was finding information; today it's avoiding being overwhelmed by too much information too rapidly.

In addition to overwhelming you with sheer quantities of information, the Internet has the potential to mislead you with biased, slanted, or simply wrong information. Your challenge as a writing student heading into the twenty-first century is to be able to separate fact from fiction, truth from half-truths and lies, valid and reliable information from propaganda. In the era of printed information, there was always someone—an editor, a reputable publishing company, a panel of experts—to decide what was worthy of publication and what wasn't. They acted as filters for you, helping to block much bad information before it ever saw the light of day. No more. You have to do it yourself.

In order to access this new endless universe of information, you need to learn new skills. When all you have is your library's card catalog and a copy of *The Readers Guide to Periodical Literature*, finding a limited amount of information is not difficult. But imagine if you opened a drawer in the card catalog and looked under a particular heading and found two million listings! You need to learn how to manipulate the strange new tools—the so-called "search engines"—the Internet provides for you.

There really has been an information explosion all around you; you must be careful not to be blown away by it.

Significance for Communication, Education, and Research

The Internet has been compared to a large worldwide library, but it's more than that. It's been compared to a communication medium like the telephone, but it's more than that as well. And it's been compared to a giant democratic publishing company that publishes everything it receives, rejecting no one. As a student, you will be able to make use of all three of these capabilities of the Internet.

For college composition classes, you will very likely be writing a variety of papers: perhaps some personal narrative, analyses of literature, persuasion pieces, and maybe a research paper or two. The actual subject matter of your writing will vary widely, so that in some sense you will have to become a master of knowledge from a number of different fields.

If you have a research paper to write, for example, your college's library catalog may be online (though the actual books and journals, for the most part, are not online), along with the other resources and databases your library makes available to its patrons. If your library offers you EBSCO or First Search or Lexis-Nexis, say, you may be able to access those sources right from your own computer, without needing to schlep down to the library itself and wait for a computer terminal to open up.

The World Wide Web has become an unimaginably large source of information, and as long as you keep your critical guard up at all times, you will find it a relatively quick and easy reference source. In literally just a few seconds at your computer, you can have at your fingertips two million or more potentially relevant sources of information. You can check a fact quickly (just how many grams of fat are in a Big Mac, anyway?) or read complete reports of research or government documents regardless of what you hear on the news. (For example, what did the Oakland School Board really say in its Ebonics proposal? The actual text is online.)

To deepen your interest and to help you think of more ideas and arguments and insights, you can listen to and even participate in any number of the tens of thousands of electronic discussions occurring worldwide over the Internet. In these topically-arranged listservs and Usenet newsgroups, everyone from the most respected experts to the least knowledgeable beginners and outsiders has the opportunity to add in their $.02 worth (or, in non-Internet-speak, two cents worth).

As you begin to organize and compose your paper, you may want to discuss some issues of either your subject matter or the actual composing process. You can email some concerns to a friend or other trusted person, someone you know who will give you good advice. It may be someone else in your class or a friend from home whose now at a different college. Many of your instructors will allow you to electronically submit rough drafts of your papers early for some feedback on your ideas and your information before the paper is actually due for a grade.

part

1

Open Topics

A very common assignment in your composition class is an open topic—in other words, you need to find something that interests you and write about it. Sometimes you will write about a personal issue that may not require any research, but sometimes your topic will lead you into research. Either way, the Internet can provide resources that will facilitate the discovery of a topic and the drafting and revising of the paper.

There are a number of ways the Internet can help you as you scout about for something to write about. First, most of the major search engines (Yahoo!, Infoseek, Excite, etc.) provide indexes of categorized information. Decide on a general topic that you think you may be interested in researching (cars, nuclear energy, domestic violence, whatever); then use that topic as your initial keyword search of the index. These index searches are useful for getting a quick overview of a topic to see if you have any interest in pursuing it further. If there's very little information available, or if the information is dated, unreliable, or even uninteresting, then you can eliminate that topic from your list of possibilities.

If you find that there's enough information on a topic to make it worth pursuing, then the next stage will be narrowing your topic. Most time your first instinct on a topic will be much too broad for the length of paper you're expected to write. A topic like "domestic violence," for example, needs a library shelf full of books to do it justice—one short research paper can't begin to say anything meaningful or insightful about that topic. So you must narrow your topic. The hierarchical index structure of sites like Yahoo! is tailor-made for this kind of narrowing. Once you've found a subject with quite a few listings underneath it, you can burrow your way down, clicking on subtopic after subtopic until you get to one that seems manageable—big enough to have some substantial information about it but small enough to examine in detail without writing hundreds of pages.

Another often-overlooked Internet resource for finding a topic of interest is Usenet newsgroups. Like WWW indexes, newsgroups are arranged hierarchically, so with your newsreader you can follow a path by clicking within a major category until you come to a specific area that interests you, and then checking over the list of subjects dealt with in the particular group. If the subjects look interesting and there seems to be a lot of discussion and followup, then you can be certain that there is a certain amount of information available and that your topic has some inherent interest to people beyond yourself (always a plus!). By dipping into the actual postings in the newsgroups you can also begin to map out what the major issues within your topic are. You can be guaranteed that a Usenet discussion will bring up far more issues and viewpoints than you could ever have thought of by yourself. Beware, however, of taking much of the actual information you find in a newsgroup as reliable. Evaluate any material you intend to quote or cite very carefully.

If your topic needs to be more personal, drawn from your own experiences and memories, you may not have to research the topic much for additional information, but you may need help with getting the flow of memories started, or filling in some gaps (how old was my grandmother on that fateful day in 1983?). For these, you can brainstorm with classmates over email or a listserv (if your instructor has set up some kind of electronic communication system for your class). And for filling in those old memories, emailing relatives is a possibility—it's cheaper than a phone call, you never miss the person or get an answering machine, and sometimes the act of writing an email response produces more thoughtful and detailed answers.

Writing about Literature

Another very common essay assignment in composition is writing about literature. You may need to find background information about an author or work of literature, or you may need to critically analyze a work or a number of works.

Most famous and classical authors have Web pages devoted to them. You can find out biographical information on the author, sometimes critical or historical analyses of the writings, and links to more resources. If you need some guidance on actually doing the critical analysis and writing the paper, a good starting point is the Western Michigan University Web site, Writing Papers of Literary Analysis: Some advice for student writers (http://www.wmich.edu/english/tchg/lit/adv/lit.papers.html). To help you master the arcane jargon of literary criticism, there's a hypertext list of terms available on the University of Victoria's UVic Writer's Guide (http://webserver.maclab.comp.uvic.ca/writersguide/Pages/MasterToc.html#Literary Terms Alpha). The Gutenberg Project is placing as many out-of-copyright texts as possible on the Internet, so

part

1

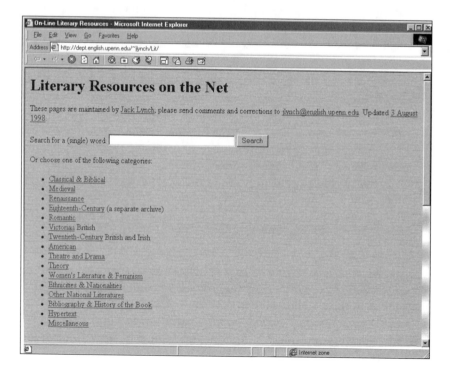

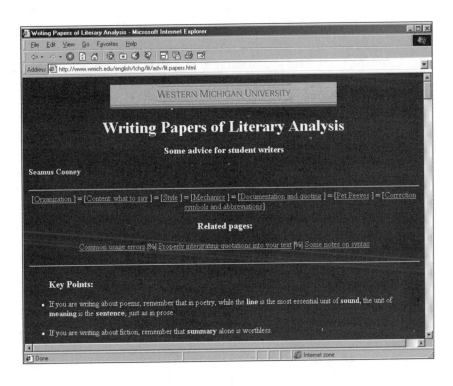

part

1

if you've lent your copy of Shakespeare to your roommate who's out of town for the weekend, you can still track down that quote from Hamlet.

Publishing and Receiving Feedback on Your Writing

The Internet is a remarkable medium—it can be both a place where you read and a place where you write, both a library and a publishing house. One very valuable use you can make of the Net in your own writing classes (in fact, in all of your classes), will be to share your writing with others before it's finalized. This is most commonly accomplished via email, but if you have access to a Web server you can actually upload your writing as a simple Web page. This is the simplest and most effective ways, since by saving your draft as an html Web page, nearly all the formatting (underlining, boldface, etc.) of the paper is retained. The downside is that not many students have access to their own Web server, though this is changing rapidly.

But by far the most prevalent way of sharing drafts, in both education and "the real world" of business and industry, is email. Despite the standards and apparent universality that mark the Internet, sending documents over email is fraught with difficulties, owing to a legion of incompatibilities: Mac and Windows, MS Word (and its many mutually-incompatible versions) and WordPerfect, quoted-printable and MIME, Base 64 and uucode and binhex. If you're sure that the person(s) receiving your document are using exactly the same resources (Word 97 on a Windows machine, for example) and both your ISP and the receiver's ISP use the same encoding/decoding scheme (Base 64, for example) then you'll have no problems. Simply "attach" your wordprocessed draft to an email message and send it on its way. If that doesn't work, try saving your draft as an "RTF" (Rich Text Format) file, a format that is close to independent of platform (Mac or Windows) and wordprocessing software. Using this format when attaching files can allow someone using WordPerfect on a Mac to read your draft written with Word 97 on a Windows machine. But even RTF is not foolproof.

Often you'll find that your draft arrives at its destination as a garbled mess of letters and unreadable characters. What to do? The answer will involve some compromises. If the text of your draft does not depend extensively on its formatting (headings, boldface, etc.) then you can settle on the lingua franca of the Internet, ASCII text. Using cut and paste, cut your text from your word processing program and then paste it into a blank email message in your email software, and send it. The message will consist of only your words and punctuation—no formatting at all other than paragraphing, but that may be satisfactory.

Redline

Your composition instructor may choose to take advantage of a WWW-based file-posting service like Redline (or you and a few friends or classmates may opt to enroll independent of any class). Redline allows you to post your paper to a central site which your classmates have access to as well. Then they can read your draft online, and post their responses and suggestions for revision online. And you can do the same for their drafts.

To use Redline, you must first subscribe and, sadly, pay (though the registration fee is small). After that, for the rest of the semester you'll have access to the service. To post your draft for others to read, you must first use your word processor to save the draft in ASCII (yes, you'll lose all your formatting). Then, go into the Redline Web site and choose "post document." (Figure 1).

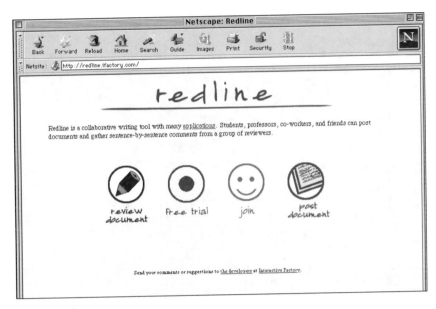

FIGURE 1

You will then be prompted for the file you wish to submit (your word processed file saved as ASCII text), the identities of those other Redline subscribers who are to have access to your draft to read and respond to them, and other choices about deadlines and reminders to your readers. Once you've done that, the persons you've designated as readers will instantly receive email notifying them that the draft is available for reading and providing them with a special access code that will allow them to read and respond to it.

To respond to others' drafts, first jot down the access code you received from the writer in your email, and go to the Redline site and choose "review document." You'll be prompted to login and enter the access code for the paper you want to read. When this is successful, you'll see the draft you want to review. Each sentence is followed by a red dot. (Figure 2)

To respond to a particular sentence or spot in the draft, click on the red dot following the sentence or section that you want to respond to. In the right hand column of your screen, you'll see the entire sentence appear; you'll be able to rewrite that sentence as a suggestion to the author, or add your own comment. When you're done paging through the entire document and commenting, you'll have the opportunity to add a final overall comment. When you indicate that you're finished, the author will receive email telling her that you've responded to her draft.

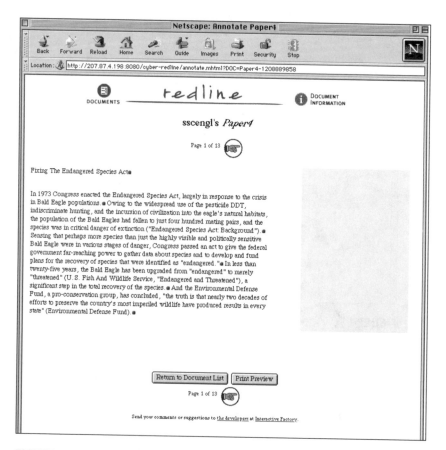

FIGURE 2

She can then check out your comments (and those of others) at her leisure.

Finding Help (OWLs)

One of the more recent developments on the Internet is the Online Writing Lab, or OWL for short. Perhaps even your own school's writing lab is online. But if it isn't, online help is still available if you can't catch your professor during her office hours and your friends are gone for the weekend and you have a paper due. Many OWLs around the country allow you to discuss your writing online with tutors, and some, especially the larger ones like those at Purdue University and the University

part

1

of Michigan, will, on a limited and time-available basis, allow your to submit drafts of your papers for feedback from the tutors. A complete listing of Writing Centers with online components is available at http://departments.colgate.edu/diw/NWCAOWLS.html.

OWLs that respond to students outside their own college allow you to email a paper or a question to their staff; in some cases they actually provide forms on the Web page itself to simplify the submission of papers or questions. If your school doesn't have a writing center, or for those times when you feel the need to have other readers of your paper (or even if you just have a simple question on *it's* vs. *its* or non-sexist language), these online writing centers may prove useful to you. (As a matter of courtesy, you of course shouldn't abuse the privilege by frequent requests for services.)

Using the Internet for Research Papers

At some point in your composition classes you'll probably have to write a research paper. With the Internet at your disposal, you're better off than your predecessors of twenty or fifty years ago, because you have almost instantaneous access to the seemingly unlimited world of information. You don't necessarily have to trudge out to the library at an inconvenient time to find your information. But on the other hand, with this abundance of easily-obtainable information comes the responsibility to sort through it, evaluate it, and synthesize it into something meaningful. Not an easy job when you have two million sources to check out!

All of the techniques above for finding a topic still apply, of course. Browsing indexes like Yahoo! is a useful tool, and Usenet groups are still provocative. Use both if you need a jump-start for ideas to write about, or to help you pinpoint a precise topic. Brainstorming online with classmates and emailing friends, relatives and experts in a field—all these will be useful for getting started and keeping the flow of ideas, insights, and information going.

In certain cases your professor may give you the option of finding something that you yourself are interested in, and researching that topic. Once you're ready to start researching and writing, the Internet will provide you with sources of information and resources for help.

part

1

Online Library Resources

Many of the standard library indexes are now available online, though they may often charge your library a fee for students to use the services. But many college and university libraries are willing to invest in the online versions of such standbys as EBSCO, First Search, InfoTrac, Encyclopedia Britannica, Lexis-Nexis, in order to provide better services for their students and to cut down on the amount of bound paper volumes they must purchase and store annually. If your library subscribes to one of these national services, they can be real time savers for you.

Most valuable will be the services offering "full-text" retrieval. This means that you will be able to read (and in many cases download and save) the full text of certain magazine and journal articles. Otherwise, you can search the index and find you the articles you need to read, but then you must go to your library and actually find the print version of the cited journal and article that you want.

Sample Search on EBSCO

EBSCO is a popular reference service available in many college libraries. It claims to provide indexes and abstracts for over 3,100 periodicals and to provide full-text search and retrieval for 1,500 of those. In addition to covering general reference sources, its main database ("Masterfile") also covers business, health, social science, education, science, humanities and news sources. Other databases, smaller but more specifically focused, are Health Source Plus, Newspaper Source, and Business Source Elite.

When you first access the EBSCO home page (remember, your library must subscribe to the service for you to be able to use it—it's not available to single users) you'll see the screen in Figure 3.

Check MasterFILE FullTEXT 1500 and click on the **ENTER** button. You'll see the screen in Figure 4. To find information from the EBSCO Masterfile database, enter your query in the "Find" box. Boolean operators are available to you as they are in the most popular Web search engines, so it's possible to construct very precise queries. You may also limit your search to only those magazines for which EBSCO has the full texts by checking the "Full Text" box. Otherwise, the search will cover all titles indexed by EBSCO. If you want a really detailed search and are prepared to wade through a good deal of tangentially-related results, you may ask EBSCO to search not only titles and abstracts but within the texts themselves for your keywords. Or you may limit your search to a particular magazine if you wish. In general, however, the default values

part

1

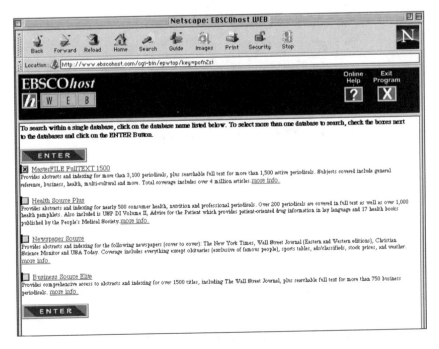

FIGURE 3

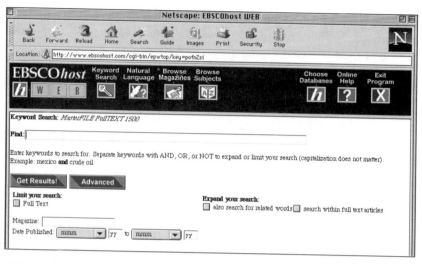

FIGURE 4

(i.e., no expanders or limiters checked) will serve you best in your quest for information.

If you're interested in writing a paper about the so-called "Year 2000 Bug," enter the phrase "Year 2000 Bug" into the Find box. Your results will look something like Figure 5.

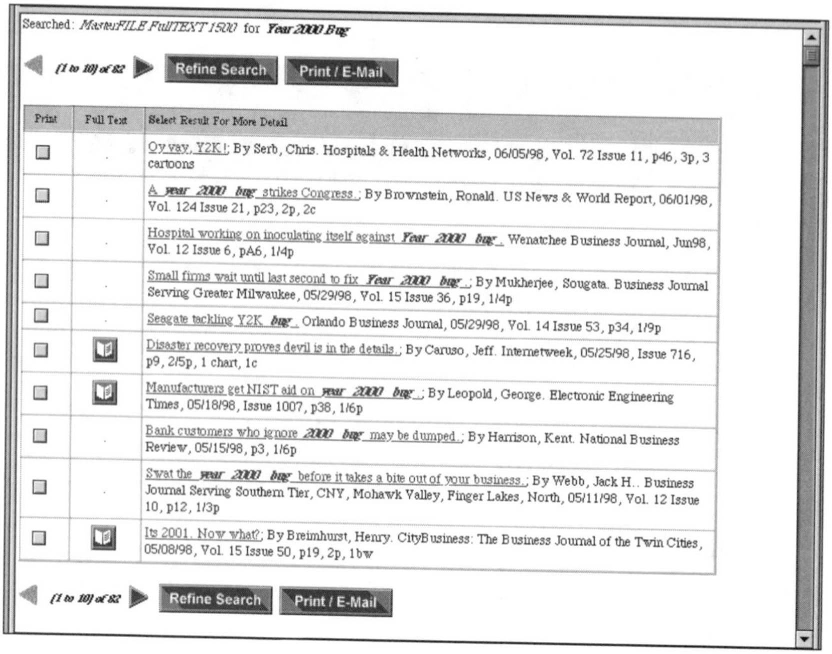

FIGURE 5

This particular search, on this particular day, turned up 82 articles pertaining to the Year 2000 Bug. The first ten are displayed. Of these ten, the three with the icon in the "Full Text" column are available in full-text form, which means you have access to the entire article online. You can read the entire article at your computer; or by clicking on the "Print/E-Mail" button you can print the article (if your computer is hooked up to a printer—not all are), you can save the text of the article on a floppy disk you've brought with you, or you can email the article to yourself (convenient if the computer you're working at is not connected to a printer and you don't have a disk with you). If the article looks potentially useful, it's best to save its text to a disk so that you'll be able to cut and paste from the text when you're writing your paper and need exact quotations from the article.

If you get lost, there's online help available on every page.

Special Cases

A few Web-based specialized research sources deserve special mention. Unlike the more generic search engines like AltaVista and HotBot, the Web sites Researchpaper.com (http://www.researchpaper.com), the Internet Public Library (http://www.ipl.org), and the Electric Library (http://www.elibrary.com) are specifically targeted for student writers of research papers.

Researchpaper.com provides help and advice throughout all stages of writing a research paper, from finding a topic to finding information to finding fellow students around the world to discuss your topic and your paper. The Electric Library is a fee-based service, but it offers a thirty-day free tryout subscription. You may try it for one research project, and if you like it, you can subscribe for a longer period of time. The Internet Public Library has a wealth of links to other online sources of information, plus it's comfortably arranged like a library.

Writing for the Internet

As a medium that is somewhere between speech and formal writing, the Internet is changing the way we think about and go about writing. The qualities that make for good essays are not necessarily the same qualities that make for good Internet writing. For example, much electronic

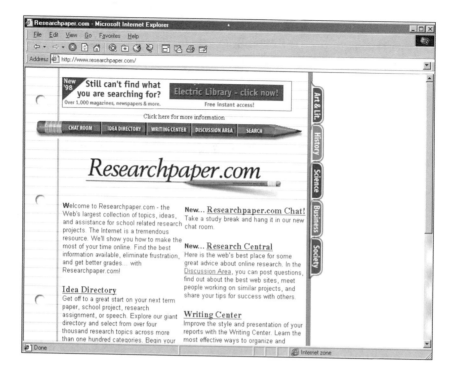

writing—email, Web pages, chat rooms, posts to Usenet—is briefer than regular writing for your college courses. And it's generally understood that electronic writing is more tentative and exploratory, a place to work out ideas in the crucible of the Internet rather than making final pronouncements on a particular issue.

Email

Your instructor may ask that you use email in a number of ways, or you may have discovered the value of email yourself. In either event there are certain conventions that need to be adhered to.

1. Be brief. Write succinctly. Let your ideas develop in the give and take of email exchanges.

2. DON'T TYPE IN ALL CAPS. This is shouting.

3. Use emoticons (smileys) to indicate irony or another tone of voice :-)

4. Don't write anything you wouldn't tape on the wall of the student center. Consider your message carefully before you hit "send." Don't

"flame" or otherwise personally disparage someone who disagrees with you.

5. Make your subject line brief but accurate.

6. For the reference of the sender, when replying to a message quote the relevant part of the sender's message.

7. When forwarding messages, put your comments before the forwarded message.

8. Use, but don't overuse, net-acceptable acronyms like BTW (by the way) or IMHO (in my humble opinion).

9. Though spelling and grammar rules are looser for such an immediate medium as the Internet, make your points clear (this means quickly double-check your sentences for gross grammatical errors, omitted words, etc.). Use your spell checker.

Listservs and Usenet

Your instructor may ask that you join a listserv (or she may actually set up for the use of you and your classmates), or she may ask you to follow a newsgroup or two. Even though listserv discussions are conducted via email, their conventions are closer to those of Usenet. Many of the rules for Usenet and listserv discussions are the same as those for email. It's particularly important in a very public medium like Usenet to remember the no-flame rule. Even though you will run across a good deal of flaming, or you may be tempted to flame someone yourself, remember the intellectual nature of what you're doing: you're engaging in serious intellectual discussion and the creation of ideas and new meanings.

A few additional rules for Usenet/listservs:

10. Don't attach files for posting to discussion groups.

11. Turn off formatting (bold, italics, anything non-ASCII) when posting.

12. Don't post personal messages from someone to a public forum like Usenet or a listserv without the person's permission, and don't post copyrighted materials.

Chats, MUDs, and MOOs

The newest implementation of technology in composition courses is the "synchronous" discussion, formats (such as chats, MUDs, MOOs) for real-time written interaction among a group of people who may or may not be in the same room. Think of them as instantaneous email: you write a message, and instantly it appears on the screen of everyone else who's participating.

The simplest and perhaps most well-known is the chat, popularized by America Online and a number of other Internet services. It basically allows for the simplest exchange of writing among a group. MUDs (Multiple User Domains) and their later incarnations MOOs (MUD, Object-Oriented) are descended from text adventure games like Dungeons and Dragons, and have been adapted for use in academia. While you won't run into any dragons or gnomes, you may run into a "note" in the "room" your instructor has set up containing the day's writing assignment, for example. MOOs go beyond simple chats by allowing you to create a character for yourself and to create and use a variety of objects in the virtual room. But at heart they are all ways of writing.

You may be wondering why, especially if you're all in the same room, you and your classmates should be writing to each other over computer networks. Why not just talk to each other? There are a number of reasons. First, and probably dearest to the heart of your composition instructor, is the fact that you're writing (this is a composition course, after all). Second, even though you're not truly anonymous in a chat or MOO (most of your classmates know who you really are, even if you've registered with a pseudonym like "Lone Ranger" or "Night Diva"), there's something about the feeling of anonymity that allows you to contribute openly and honestly and productively to the class discussion. Have you ever sat in a class with something that you thought was important and worthwhile that you wanted to say, while the class was being dominated by the teacher and the two smartest (or loudest or pushiest) students? In a synchronous chat, you have that opportunity to be heard. Most students will say that they're much less inhibited and more likely to contribute in a chat or MOO. Finally, MOOs and chats are real writing. They're not dull papers written on a topic that you don't care about for a single person, the teacher. You get a taste of writing when real people actually read what you've written and care about what you say and respond to you, even if it's to question or dispute or support you.

The general conventions and expectations of online chatting are the essentially the same as for the other forms of online writing: keep your individual messages brief, remember courtesy and intellectual respect for your classmates' ideas, and pause briefly before you hit the "send" button to consider the effects of your words. But you needn't worry too much, for you'll immediately see the effects of your words on your screen as your classmates reply—for better or worse.

A few simple commands to maneuver in a MOO:

- To speak on a MOO, precede your message with a quotation mark (") or the word *say*
- To emote, precede your verbs (e.g., laughs, smiles, blushes) with a colon
- To get help online, type help
- To quit, type @quit

Composing Web Pages

Though it may not seem to have much to do with a composition class, composing Web pages is becoming more popular as an assignment. You may be asked to (or you may want to) create a Web page on a particular topic—a favorite author, historical event or period, or other topic of interest to you. As with all writing, composing a Web page requires you to understand your audience and to carefully select and arrange your material to make your point. But unlike other writing tasks, writing for the Web will include graphics and, in some cases, other forms of multimedia.

Fortunately, you have the advantage of not having to learn the language of the Web—html. Most modern word processors have the capability of turning wordprocessed documents into Web pages, though they are limited in what they can do. But for more advanced or complex Web compositions, there are many software packages (e.g., Microsoft Front-Page, Adobe PageMill) available today to let you compose your pages the way you want them, and then invisibly write the necessary html language for you.

Some initial pointers for writing effective Web pages:

1. Be sure you have a reason to create the page. Again, this is real writing: if your page is actually placed on a server somewhere for the whole world to see, there will be literally millions of people who may see your page. Don't waste their time. The rule is "value-added"—if you're not adding anything of value to the WWW, don't add anything at all.

2. Use graphical (and other more exotic multimedia) material sparingly, and effectively. Remember, even if you are working on a high-speed network at your school, millions of people still have slow modems at home. In the split-second world of the Internet, they will not wait

part

1

minutes for your graphics or Quicktime movies, no matter how wonderful or appropriate they are.

3. Think hypertextually. Keep your first page of text brief (one or two screenfuls at the most) and make links to related pages (your own, or others you've found while researching on the Web) for further explanation or discussion of your material.

4. Make navigation easy. Provide links back and forth to all other levels of your site.

5. Unless you have a good reason not to, avoid trendy enhancements, for the most part: frames, animated GIFs, etc. (Note: there is no good reason to use the "blink" feature!)

6. For further info, consult the online Yale HTML Style Guide (http://info.med.yale.edu/caim/manual/contents.html)

Final Words

 part
1

It's almost a cliché to say the the Internet is revolutionizing writing and reading, the very foundations of college composition courses. But cliché or not, it's true. Every aspect of reading and writing has undergone some change since the days of the publishing houses and the local newspapers. The opportunities for new literacies are everywhere, as is a full set of new challenges and problems and frustrations. This is the new college composition course.

Critical Evaluation

Where Seeing Is Not Always Believing

Typical research resources, such as journal articles, books, and other scholarly works, are reviewed by a panel of experts before being published. At the very least, any reputable publisher takes care to assure that the author is who he or she claims to be and that the work being published represents a reasoned and informed point of view. When anyone can post anything in a Web site or to a newsgroup, the burden of assessing the relevance and accuracy of what you read falls to you. Rumors quickly grow into facts on the Internet simply because stories can spread so rapidly that the "news" seems to be everywhere. Because the Internet leaves few tracks, in no time it's impossible to tell whether you are reading independent stories or the merely same story that's been around the world two or three times. Gathering information on the Internet may be quick, but verifying the quality of information requires a serious commitment.

Approach researching via the Internet with confidence, however, and not with trepidation. You'll find it an excellent workout for your critical evaluation skills; no matter what career you pursue, employers value an employee who can think critically and independently. Critical thinking is also the basis of problem solving, another ability highly valued by the business community. So, as you research your academic projects, be assured that you're simultaneously developing lifelong expertise.

It's Okay to Be Critical of Others

The first tip for successful researching on the Internet is to always consider your source. A Web site's URL often alerts you to the sponsor of the site. CNN or MSNBC are established news organizations, and you can give the information you find at their sites the same weight you would give to their cablecasts. Likewise, major newspapers operate Web sites with articles reprinted from their daily editions or expanded stories written expressly for the Internet. On the other hand, if you're unfamiliar with the source, treat the information the way you would any new data. Look for specifics—"66 percent of all voters" as opposed to "most voters"—and for information that can be verified—a cited report in another medium or information accessible through a Web site hosted by a credible sponsor—as opposed to generalities or unverifiable claims. Look for independent paths to the same information. This can involve careful use of search engines or visits to newsgroups with both similar and opposing viewpoints. Make sure that the "independent" information you find is truly independent. In newsgroups don't discount the possibility of multiple postings, or that a posting in one group is nothing more than a quotation from a posting in another. Ways to verify independent paths include following sources (if any) back to their origins, contacting the person posting a message and asking for clarification, or checking other media for verification.

In many cases, you can use your intuition and common sense to raise your comfort level about the soundness of the information. With both list servers and newsgroups, it's possible to lurk for a while to develop a feeling for the authors of various postings. Who seems the most authoritarian, and who seems to be "speaking" from emotion or bias? Who seems to know what he or she is talking about on a regular basis? Do these people cite their sources of information (a job or affiliation

part

1

perhaps)? Do they have a history of thoughtful, insightful postings, or do their postings typically contain generalities, unjustifiable claims, or flames? On Web sites, where the information feels more anonymous, there are also clues you can use to test for authenticity. Verify who's hosting the Web site. If the host or domain name is unfamiliar to you, perhaps a search engine can help you locate more information. Measure the tone and style of the writing at the site. Does it seem consistent with the education level and knowledge base necessary to write intelligently about the subject?

When offering an unorthodox point of view, good authors supply facts, figures, and quotes to buttress their positions, expecting readers to be skeptical of their claims. Knowledgeable authors on the Internet follow these same commonsense guidelines. Be suspicious of authors who expect you to agree with their points of view simply because they've published them on the Internet. In one-on-one encounters, you frequently judge the authority and knowledge of the speaker using criteria you'd be hard pressed to explain. Use your sense of intuition on the Internet, too.

As a researcher (and as a human being), the job of critical thinking requires a combination of healthy skepticism and rabid curiosity. Newsgroups and Web sites tend to focus narrowly on single issues (newsgroups more so than Web sites). Don't expect to find a torrent of opposing views on newsgroup postings; their very nature and reason for existence dampens free-ranging discussions. A newsgroup on *The X-Files* might argue about whether extraterrestrials exist but not whether the program is the premier television show on the air today. Such a discussion would run counter to the purposes of the newsgroup and would be a violation of netiquette. Anyone posting such a message would be flamed, embarrassed, ignored, or otherwise driven away. Your research responsibilities include searching for opposing views by visiting a variety of newsgroups and Web sites. A help here is to fall back on the familiar questions of journalism: who, what, when, where, and why.

part

1

- ■ **Who** else might speak knowledgeably on this subject? Enter that person's name into a search engine. You might be surprised to find whose work is represented on the Web. (For fun, one of the authors entered the name of a rock-and-roll New York radio disk jockey into MetaCrawler and was amazed to find several pages devoted to the DJ, including sound clips of broadcasts dating back to the sixties, along with a history of his theme song.)

■ **What** event might shed more information on your topic? Is there a group or organization that represents your topic? Do they hold an annual conference? Are synopses of presentations posted on the sponsoring organization's Web site?

■ **When** do events happen? Annual meetings or seasonal occurrences can help you isolate newsgroup postings of interest.

■ **Where** might you find this information? If you're searching for information on wines, for example, check to see if major wine-producing regions, such as the Napa Valley in California or the Rhine Valley in Germany, sponsor Web sites. These may point you to organizations or information that don't show up in other searches. Remember, Web search engines are fallible; they don't find every site you need.

■ **Why** is the information you're searching for important? The answer to this question can lead you to related fields. New drugs, for example, are important not only to victims of diseases but to drug companies and the FDA as well.

part

1

Approach assertions you read from a skeptic's point of view. See if they stand up to critical evaluation or if you're merely emotionally attached to them. Imagine "What if . . . ?" or "What about . . . ?" scenarios that may disprove or at least call into question what you're reading. Try following each assertion you pull from the Internet with the phrase, "On the other hand. . . ." Because you can't leave the sentence hanging, you'll be forced to finish it, and this will help get you into the habit of critically examining information.

These are, of course, the same techniques critical thinkers have employed for centuries, only now you are equipped with more powerful search tools than past researchers may have ever imagined. In the time it took your antecedents to formulate their questions, you can search dozens of potential information sources. You belong to the first generation of college students to enjoy both quantity and quality in its research, along with a wider perspective on issues and the ability to form personal opinions after reasoning from a much wider knowledge base. Certainly, the potential exists for the Internet to grind out a generation of intellectual robots, "thinkers" who don't think but who regurgitate information from many sources. Technology always has its good and bad aspects. However, we also have the potential to become some of the most well-informed thinkers in the history of the world, thinkers who are not only articulate but confident that their opinions have been distilled from a range of views, processed by their own personalities, beliefs, and biases. This is one of the aspects of the Internet that makes this era such an exciting combination of humanism and technology.

part

1

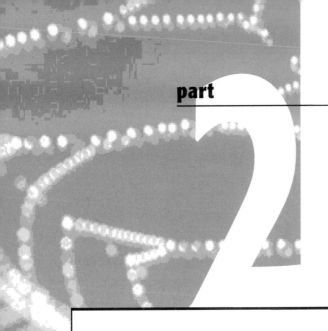

Internet Activities for College Composition

1. Find an email discussion list (listserv) that you might be interested in. Lurk for a week or two. Can you find its FAQ? How would you characterize the tone of most of the postings? Are controversial issues tackled? Are there any flames? If so, for what reason? What seems to be a significant taboo on this list?

2. Do the same for a Usenet newsgroup. What are the differences you see between the newsgroup and the email list?

3. If anyone seems particularly knowledgeable or authoritative on either the list or the newsgroup, after a couple of weeks, send him or her a private email asking for clarification or further expansion of some point he or she made. Do you get an answer? If so, how would you describe the answer?

4. In a thread from either the newsgroup or the listserv, try to find an example of:

   a. Flaming

   b. An unsupported assertion

   c. A misreading of someone's post

   d. An especially convincing argument

   e. An obviously biased poster

5. Find two different lists or newsgroups dealing with roughly the same topic. Contrast them: the tone, the willingness to either disagree or

engage in verbal combat, the unwritten and unspoken assumptions behind the postings.

6. What is the difference between a search engine and a directory (aka index)?

7. What are the parts of a URL? Give an example of a URL and explain what each part means.

8. What is a query?

9. Explain in your own words how the AND operator limits a category and the OR operator expands a category.

10. Is the Boolean phrase "(coffee AND cream) OR sugar" the same as "coffee AND (cream or sugar)"? Why or why not?

11. Explain in your own words how Boolean operators and other logical operators work in a query. Give an example of a complex query, using both Boolean and other logicals, and explain how it will be read by a search engine. What kinds of information do you expect it to find?

12. Use that query in your favorite search engine. Are there any surprises?

13. Enter a simple search with minimal Boolean operators into Excite. How many documents does it find? Enter the same search into AltaVista. How many documents does it find? How do the two searches contrast?

14. Begin keeping a personal chart for yourself of the strengths and weaknesses of each of the major search engines. Keep adding to it as you gain more experience with Web searching.

15. Browse the Yahoo! directory (**http://www.yahoo.com/**). Find a general topic you think might be worth pursuing in a research paper; follow Yahoo!'s links to narrow that topic down and to find some initial sites where potentially useful information may be stored.

The Warmups

Let's begin warming up with some practice queries and Boolean phrases.

1. Compose a Boolean phrase that describes a group of desserts which are pies and which are either apple or peach.

part 2

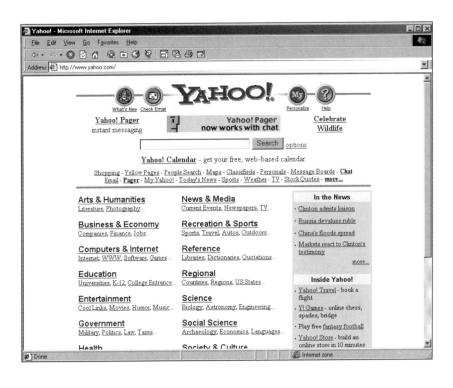

_____

_____

_____

2. Compose a Boolean phrase that describes a group of desserts which are pies of all kinds except cherry.

_____

_____

_____

3. Construct a query for AltaVista that will find, in the first ten hits, when Galileo was born. Try it; refine it if necessary.

_____

_____

_____

4. Construct a query for AltaVista that finds sites opposed to the Endangered Species Act.

_____

_____

_____

5. Try the query from question 4. What do you find? How can you refine your search to more closely focus on the goal?

_____

_____

_____

The Hunt (WWW)

part

2

In the early days of the Internet, there was a monthly contest called "The Internet Hunt," in which one of the few users of the Net would pose a problem for the other few users, and the first one to find the answer on the Internet (and provide documentation for how she did it) won. Once the Internet grew to hundreds of thousands and finally tens of millions users, the contest became unwieldy and it was discontinued. But it was a good idea—many a budding Internet researcher cut teeth on this contest.

So for practice, here is a list of new "Internet Hunts" for you to try out your new research skills. For each question, provide

1. The answer

2. The URL where you found the answer

3. The process you used (most likely, the query phrase and the search engine used, and perhaps the intermediate links you clicked on)

All of these questions will be answerable from the World Wide Web (or occasionally from its predecessors Gopher or FTP—all accessible via your Web browser.) There will often be a variety of correct answers to parts 2 and 3—the Web is notorious for providing multiple paths to the same points.

Questions

1. Where is Karl Marx buried (city, country, cemetery)?

   Answer:

   _____

   _____

   _____

   URL:

   _____

   _____

   _____

   Process:

   _____

   _____

   _____

part

2

2. What is the name of the Greek astronomer who calculated the circumference of the Earth over 1,500 years before Columbus sailed?

   Answer:

   _____

   _____

   _____

   URL:

   _____

   _____

   _____

   Process:

   _____

   _____

   _____

3. According to Grant himself, what does the middle initial "S" stand for in "Ulysses S. Grant"? (Note: it's not "Simpson.")

Answer:

_____

_____

_____

URL:

_____

_____

_____

Process:

_____

_____

_____

part

2

4. How many blue whales are left on planet Earth?

Answer:

_____

_____

_____

URL:

_____

_____

_____

Process:

_____

_____

_____

5. How many hours a day does the average American child watch television?

Answer:

_____

_____

_____

URL:

_____

_____

_____

Process:

_____

_____

_____

part

2

6. What woman led the fight to clean up Love Canal in the 1970s?

Answer:

_____

_____

_____

URL:

_____

_____

_____

Process:

_____

_____

_____

7. Who coined the term "rock and roll"?

Answer:

_____

_____

_____

URL:

_____

_____

_____

Process:

_____

_____

_____

part
2

8. In what year did it become illegal for employers to discriminate against people with physical disabilities?

Answer:

_____

_____

_____

URL:

_____

_____

_____

Process:

_____

_____

_____

9. Browse the Yahoo! directories (not its Web-search function) for this one: What percentage of the population of Nepal is under the age of 18?

Answer:

_____

_____

_____

URL:

_____

_____

_____

Process:

_____

_____

_____

part

2

10. How many times did Robert Frost win the Pulitzer Prize?

Answer:

_____

_____

_____

URL:

_____

_____

_____

Process:

_____

_____

_____

For Discussion

Share the results in class with others. Did you all find the answers?

If someone couldn't find one, why? What was he or she doing wrong?

As a class, begin to formulate some helpful tips for finding Internet resources that seem to work for the whole class.

How many different sites did your class find with the same answer to any particular question?

And finally, did others in the class find different answers to the same question? (Many sites, for example, repeat without comment the incorrect information about Ulysses S. Grant's middle name being "Simpson"— would you have stopped after the first site that said that, if you hadn't been told that it was incorrect?) How do you interpret the different answers to the same question?

part

2

A Closer Look at Hunting

Now try this:

Use the same relatively complex search query in three or four different search engines (or as close to the same as the particular engine's rules allow).

The Query:

_____

_____

Run the searches on the same day. What do you find?

Engine _____

Number of Hits _____

URL of First (i.e., "most relevant") hit _____

_____

Engine _____

Number of Hits _____

URL of First (i.e., "most relevant") hit _____

_____

Engine _____

Number of Hits _____

URL of First (i.e., "most relevant") hit _____

_____

Engine _____

Number of Hits _____

URL of First (i.e., "most relevant") hit _____

_____

part

2

Citation Exercise

Write the "Works Cited" entry for one of the sites above in perfect MLA format.

_____

_____

_____

_____

_____

Do the same one in perfect APA format.

_____

_____

_____

_____

_____

For Class Discussion

There very likely are huge differences in the information found. What are they? How do you explain them?

Do any of the engines miss what appears to be an extremely relevant site that another (or most) of the engines find?

Can you draw any inferences about the relative strengths and weakness of each search engine. Is more always better? Is less always better?

Can you think of any situations where you would prefer one engine over another?

What do you wish the engines could do that they don't do?

Beyond Search Engines

part

2

Using the resources from Part III (following) but not using any of the search engines:

1. Find the complete text of a poem or play by a British author who lived before 1700.

2. Find a Web site devoted to an author you're reading in your composition class.

3. Find the meaning of "cerumen" using an online dictionary.

4. What does the acronym SPELL stand for?

5. What's wrong with this sentence: "Every dog must have it's day"? Where did you find the answer?

6. Find the text of Maya Angelou's poem read at the 1993 inauguration of President Clinton.

7. In Aristotle's *On Interpretation,* what must he first define?

8. What's the rule in English grammar for forming the possessive of a singular noun that ends in *s*?

9. The quote "We are such stuff as dreams are made of" is actually a misquote. What is the correct quote, and where is it found?

More Composition Activities

1. Create a small Web site based on the topic of one of your writing assignments from your composition class.

2. Find the email address of a writer you've read (or read about) in your composition class. Send him or her an email with a question or comment on the reading. Do you get an answer?

3. Get the email addresses of a few of your classmates and submit a draft of a paper you're working on to Redline. Have them respond. How helpful are services like this?

4. When you have a question of grammar and usage in your writing, submit it to one of the OWLs. How helpful and authoritative is the answer you receive?

Resources for Internet Research on Composition

Search Engines

AltaVista

`http://altavista.digital.com/`

Allows both simple and advanced searches of WWW and Usenet; fast and powerful.

Ask Jeeves

`http://www.askjeeves.com`

A very interesting search engine that allows plain English questions.

Britannica Internet Guide

`http://www.ebig.com/`

From the Encyclopedia Britannica people; evaluates, rates, and limits findings.

DejaNews

`http://www.dejanews.com`

Searches Usenet newsgroups.

Excite

`http://www.excite.com/`

An extensive multipurpose finder of information; includes a Web search engine, a directory, and other lookups; now allied with America Online.

HotBot

`http://www.hotbot.com/`

Powerful and customizable Web and Usenet search engine.

Infoseek

`http://www.infoseek.com/`

Allows searches of WWW, email addresses, Usenet, and newswires. Also includes a directory.

Lycos

`http://www.lycos.com/`

Web search engine and more: directory, graphics, PeopleFind, StockFind, Maps, etc.

Magellan

`http://www.mckinley.com/`

A large collection of pre-reviewed sites (special "Green Light" database excludes all sites with adult content), along with a directory.

Open Text

`http://index.opentext.net/`

WWW searches; in Power Search mode, provides menus for Boolean search operators; simple to use.

WebCrawler

`http://www.webcrawler.com/`

A quick and simple to use Web search engine and directory.

Yahoo!

`http://www.yahoo.com/`

Both a full-fledged WWW search engine and the most famous directory for browsing.

Fee-Based Research Services

part 2

Brainwave

`http://www.n2kbrainwave.com/`

Searches Business and Company Information, Copyrights, Patents and Trademarks, Medicine, News, People and Biographies, Science and Technology, Social Science, Government and Education.

Electric Library

`http://www.elibrary.com/`

Allows plain English searches of more than 150 full-text newspapers and 800 fulltext magazines; free 30-day subscription.

Lexis-Nexis

`http://www.lexisnexis.com`

Online legal, news, and business information services.

UnCover

`http://www.carl.org/`

A periodical index and document delivery (by fax) service.

General Directories

Berkeley Digital Library

`http://sunsite.berkeley.edu/cgi-bin/welcome.pl/`

The online collection at the University of California; searchable.

Complete Reference to Usenet Newsgroups

`http://www.tile.net/tile/news/index.html`

A searchable listing of Usenet groups.

part
2

ERIC Clearinghouse on Information and Technology

`http://ericir.syr.edu/`

The WWW starting point for the Educational Resources Clearinghouse.

Gopher Jewels

`gopher://cwis.usc.edu:70/11/Other_Gophers_and_`
`Information_Resources/Gopher-Jewels`

An extremely thorough directory of Gopher sites, arranged hierarchically.

Internet Public Library

`http://www.ipl.org`

A directory of Web information arranged like a public library.

InfoSurf: E-Journals and E-Zines

`http://www.library.ucsb.edu/mags/mags.html`

A categorically arranged list of magazines and journals available electronically.

LIBCAT

`http://www.metronet.lib.mn.us/lc/lc1.html`

Comprehensive guide to libraries (United States and worldwide) that have Internet presence.

Libweb: Library Servers via WWW

`http://sunsite.Berkeley.EDU/Libweb/`

Directory of online libraries in 62 countries; searchable by location or affiliation.

LISTSERV Lists Search

`http://tile.net/listserv/`

A searchable listing of email discussion groups (listservs).

Social Science Information Gateway

`http://sosig.esrc.bris.ac.uk`

A comprehensive listing of social science information sources available electronically worldwide.

Supreme Court Decisions

`http://www.law.cornell.edu/supct/`

A searchable database of recent Supreme Court decisions.

Voice of the Shuttle: Web Page for Humanities Research

`http://humanitas.ucsb.edu/`

An amazingly comprehensive directory of humanities-oriented Web pages.

WWW Virtual Library

`http://www.w3.org/pub/DataSources/bySubject/Overview.html`

One of the first directories of Web sites, and still one of the most comprehensive.

part

2

Desktop References

Acronym and Abbreviation List

`http://www.ucc.ie/info/net/acronyms/`

Searchable list of acronyms; also reversible to search for acronym from a keyword.

The Alternative Dictionaries

`http://www.notam.uio.no/~hcholm/altlang/`

Dictionary of slang and expressions you most likely won't find in a normal dictionary; all entries are submitted by users.

CIA World Factbook

`http://www.odci.gov/cia/publications/factbook/`

Every hard fact about every country in the world.

Computing Dictionary

`http://wombat.doc.ic.ac.uk/`

Dictionary of computing terms; often technical.

Hypertext Webster Interface

`http://c.gp.cs.cmu.edu:5103/prog/webster`

A searchable dictionary.

The King James Bible

`http://etext.virginia.edu/kjv.browse.html`

In addition to a searchable KJV, this site provides a side-by-side comparison of the King James and the Revised Standard.

The Holy Qur'an

`http://www.utexas.edu/students/amso/quran_html/`

Searchable and downloadable English translation.

Quotations Page

http://www.starlingtech.com/quotes/

Search for that quotation by keyword.

Roget's Thesaurus

http://humanities.uchicago.edu/forms_unrest/ROGET.html

An online searchable version of the venerable book of synonyms.

Scholes Library Electronic Reference Desk

http://scholes.alfred.edu/Ref.html

An index of "ready reference" sources.

Shakespeare Glossary

http://english-server.hss.cmu.edu/langs/
shakespeare-glossary.txt

Alphabetically-arranged text file of words from Shakespeare; not a concordance.

Writing Help

Allyn and Bacon's CompSite

http://www.abacon.com/compsite/

An interactive meeting place for teachers and students to share resources and work on projects.

Anti-Pedantry Page: Singular "Their" in Jane Austen and Elsewhere

http://uts.cc.utexas.edu/~churchh/austheir.html

A compilation of famous writers who've ignored the singular "their" rule.

Bartlett's Familiar Quotations

http://www.cc.columbia.edu/acis/bartleby/bartlett/

1901 edition. Searchable.

Capitalization

http://sti.larc.nasa.gov/html/Chapt4/Chapt4_TOC.html

According to NASA's Handbook.

Critique Partner Connections

http://members.tripod.com/PetalsofLife/cpc.html

A place to find a writing partner for help by email.

Dakota State University Online Writing Lab (OWL)

http://www.dsu.edu/departments/liberal/cola/OWL/

An Online Writing Lab that provides writing help via email.

DeVry Online Writing Support Center

http://www.devry-phx.edu/lrnresrc/dowsc/

Resources for integrating the Internet into your college composition classes.

An Elementary Grammar

http://www.hiway.co.uk/~ei/intro.html

Twenty-two sections of moderately technical discussions of grammatical topics from The English Institute.

Elements of Style

http://www.cc.columbia.edu/acis/bartleby/strunk/

Will Strunk's 1918 classic.

English Grammar FAQ as posted to alt.usage.english

http://www-unix.lsa.umich.edu/ling/jlawler/aue/

Answers to common grammar questions from linguist John Lawler.

part
2

A Glossary of Rhetorical Terms with Examples

`http://www.uky.edu/ArtsSciences/Classics/rhetoric.html`

Forty five rhetorical terms (Alliteration to Zeugma) with links to classical text for examples.

Grammar and Style Notes

`http://www.english.upenn.edu:80/~jlynch/grammar.html`

Alphabetically arranged guide to topics in grammar and style.

A Handbook of Terms for Discussing Poetry

`http://www.cc.emory.edu/ENGLISH/classes/Handbook/Handbook.html`

Compiled by students at Emory University.

HyperGrammar

`http://www.uottawa.ca/academic/arts/writcent/hypergrammar/intro.html`

Hypertext grammar course/handbook from the University of Ottawa.

Inklings

`http://192.41.39.106/inklings/`

A biweekly newsletter for writers on the Net.

The "It's" vs. "Its" page

`http://www.rain.org/~gshapiro/its.html`

The difference between the two homophones.

The King's English

`http://www.columbia.edu/acis/bartleby/fowler/`

Full text of H. W. Fowler's 1908 classic on English, Victorian-style.

part

2

Nebraska Center for Writers

http://mockingbird.creighton.edu/NCW/

Online resource for writers of poetry, fiction, and creative non-fiction.

On-line English Grammar

http://www.edunet.com/english/grammar/

Especially suited for non-native speakers of English; includes some sound files.

Online Writery

http://www.missouri.edu/~wleric/writery.html

"The conversation zone for writers"; tutors and writers meet online and discuss writing.

Paradigm: Online Writing Assistant

http://www.idbsu.edu/english/cguilfor/paradigm/

Almost a complete writing textbook online.

PEN Home

http://www.pen.org/

The home page of PEN, the professional association of writers and editors.

Poets and Writers Inc. Home Page

http://www.pw.org/

Support for professional writers and those who would be professional writers.

Politics and the English Language

gopher://dept.english.upenn.edu/00/Courses/Lynch3/orwell

Full text of George Orwell's plea for clarity in writing and thinking.

part 2

Punctuation

`http://sti.larc.nasa.gov/html/Chapt3/Chapt3-TOC.html`

According to NASA.

The Rhetoric Page at SDSM&T

`http://www.sdsmt.edu/www/rhetoric/rhetoric.htnl`

Links to writing resources appropriate for both students and faculty.

University of Michigan OWL

`http://www.lsa.umich.edu/ecb/OWL/owl.html`

Receive advice about your writing via email, link to other writing resources, or, if you're in Ann Arbor, make an appointment for a face-to-face tutoring session.

The Word Detective

`http://www.word-detective.com/`

Online version of the newspaper column answering questions about words.

Rensselaer Writing Center Handouts

`http://www.rpi.edu/dept/llc/writecenter/web/handouts.html`

A collection of handouts on writing topics from "abstracts" to "writing with gender-fair language."

Undergraduate Writing Center

`http://www.utexas.edu/depts/uwc/public_html/`

Services restricted to University of Texas students and staff; links to resources for writers.

The University of Victoria's Hypertext Writer's Guide

`http://webserver.maclab.comp.uvic.ca/writersguide/welcome.html`

Hypertext guides to writing and literature.

part

2

LEO: Literacy Education Online

http://leo.stcloud.msus.edu/

Help with "what's bothering you about your writing."

BGSU Online Writing Lab

gopher://gopher.bgsu.edu/11/Departments/write/

A Gopher site with downloadable grammar and writing tips.

English as a Second Language

http://www.lang.uiuc.edu/r-115/esl/

Bills itself as the starting point for learning English as a Second Language online. Includes visual and auditory resources, as well as a 24-hour help center.

Main Writing Guide

http://www.english.uiuc.edu/cws/wworkshop/mainmenu.html

Three complete online handbooks for writing.

Non-Sexist Language

http://mickey.la.psu.edu/~chayton/eng202b/nonsex.htm

Tips for avoiding sexist language, based on National Council of Teachers of English guidelines.

Purdue On-Line Writing Lab

http://owl.english.purdue.edu/

An extensive source of online help for writers, including professional help to specific questions by email.

Researchpaper.com

http://www.researchpaper.com/

An impressive compendium of research-paper help, including live chat rooms.

Tips and Resources for Writers

http://www.olywa.net/peregrine/index.html

Materials for professional writers that are appropriate for beginners as well.

The Writer's Depot

http://members.aol.com/WritersD/index.htm

For a fee, professional writers and editors will critique your work.

Writers' Workshop: Online Resources for Writers

http://www.english.uiuc.edu/cws/wworkshop/
writer.html

A directory of online writing help at the University of Illinois at Urbana–Champaign.

part

2

Writing Centers Online

http://departments.colgate.edu/diw/NWCAOWLS.html

A directory of writing centers nationwide who have online presences.

Writing Papers of Literary Analysis: Some Advice for Student Writers

http://www.wmich.edu/english/tchg/lit/adv/lit.
papers.html

From Western Michigan University.

Writing for the Internet

Everything E-Mail

http://everythingemail.net/

Everything you ever wanted to know about email.

NCSA Beginner's Guide to HTML

http://www.ncsa.uiuc.edu/General/Internet/WWW/
HTMLPrimer.html

For those times when you have to tinker under the hood of your Web pages.

MOO Help

http://www.du.org/dumoo/moohelps.htm

Basic MOO techniques and commands from Diversity University.

Student Web Pages

http://www2.haverford.edu/acc/training/webtrain/
students/studenttour.html

Student-oriented guide from Haverford College.

User Guide to Netiquette

http://www.pepperdine.edu/ir/UserServices/helpdesk/
usergide/netiquet.htm

How to behave, electronically speaking.

WWWScribe: Web Resources for Writers

http://www.wwwscribe.com/

Writing for the WWW, along with using the Internet as a research and communication tool.

Evaluating Information on the Internet

Checklist for Evaluating Web Sites

http://www.canisius.edu/canhp/canlib/webcrit.htm

Tips from the Canisius University Library.

part 2

Criteria for Evaluation of Internet Information Resources

`http://www.vuw.ac.nz/dlis/courses/847/m2resev1.html`

From an online Internet resources course from Victoria University, New Zealand.

Critically Analyzing Information

`http://www.library.cornell.edu/okuref/research/skill26.htm`

Not specifically devoted to Internet information sources.

Evaluating Internet Information

`http://milton.mse.jhu.edu:8001/research/education/net.html`

Specific guidance from Johns Hopkins University.

Evaluating Internet Research Sources

`http://www.sccu.edu/faculty/R_Harris/evalu8it.htm`

A comprehensive essay, not just a checklist.

Evaluating Internet Resources

`http://www.snymor.edu/~drewwe/workshop/evalint.htm`

A checklist, links to more resources, and a bibliography.

Evaluating Quality on the Net

`http://www.tiac.net/users/hope/findqual.html`

An excellent and continually evolving paper from Hope Tillman, Babson College.

Internet Navigator—Evaluating Internet Information

`http://sol.slcc.edu/lr/navigator/discovery/eval.html`

From Salt Lake Community College's online Internet resources course.

part

2

Internet Tutorial: Evaluating Internet Resources

http://www.liunet.edu/cwis/cwp/library/internet/
evaluate.htm

A short document from Long Island University.

Thinking Critically about World Wide Web Resources

http://www.library.ucla.edu/libraries/college/
instruct/critical.htm

A concise outline, from UCLA.

Specialized Web Sites

Abortion and Reproductive Rights Internet Resources

http://www.caral.org/abortion.html

An extensive set of links to information both pro-choice and pro-life.

Alex: A Catalog of Electronic Texts on the Internet

http://www.lib.ncsu.edu/staff/morgan/alex/alex-index.
html

A listing of full-length texts available on the Internet.

African Americana

http://www.lib.lsu.edu/hum/african.html

A moderately extensive directory of Web sites (and more) dealing with
the African American experience.

American Poetry Hyper-bibliography

http://www.hti.umich.edu/english/amverse/hyperbib.
html

A Web-based guide to American poetry, searchable on author or title.

American Studies Web

`http://www.georgetown.edu/crossroads/asw/`

A good jumping off point for studies in Americana.

AstroWeb: Astronomy/Astrophysics on the Internet

`http://www.cv.nrao.edu/fits/www/astronomy.html`

An extensive directory of links and a searchable database of topics in astronomy.

The Business Communication World Wide Web Resource Center

`http://idt.net/~reach/Lance/lance-cohen.html`

A guide for business writing, with links to other online resources.

National Center for Education Statistics

`http://nces.ed.gov/pubsearch/index.html`

Department of Education site containing statistics on education in the United States.

Essays in History—University of Virginia

`http://www.lib.virginia.edu/journals/EH/EH.html`

Full text of the journal *Essays in History* issues since 1990.

FAQ: How to Find People's E-mail Addresses

`http://www.cis.ohio-state.edu/hypertext/faq/usenet/finding-addresses/faq.html`

A guide to the often frustrating process of finding an email address.

Fedworld Information Network

`http://www.fedworld.gov/`

The searchable gateway to the huge information resources of the federal government.

part
2

Feminist Activist Resources on the Net

`http://www.igc.org/women/feminist.html`

A compilation of useful links to feminist resources.

GPO Access Databases

`http://www.access.gpo.gov/su_docs/aces/aaces002.html`

Another guide to government publications, online and print versions (with instructions for ordering print documents).

The Human-Languages Page

`http://www.june29.com/HLP/`

A huge compendium of links to resources in language.

Internet Movie Database

`http://us.imdb.com/`

A keyword-searchable database of everything you ever wanted to know about movies.

Journals

`http://english-server.hss.cmu.edu/journals/`

Alphabetical listing (with links) to hundreds of journals, both print-based and electronic, that have a Web presence; from Carnegie-Mellon's Humanities Server.

Library of Congress

`http://lcweb.loc.gov/`

The jumping off point for the Library's online resources; not the whole Library itself, however.

Liszt

`http://www.liszt.com`

A searchable and browsable guide to listservs (email discussion lists).

Media History Project

http://www.mediahistory.com/

A gateway to information on communications and media studies; searchable.

NASA Spacelink

http://spacelink.msfc.nasa.gov/

NASA's fulfillment of its obligation to disseminate all the information it gathers through space exploration.

National Center for Health Statistics

http://www.cdc.gov/nchswww/default.htm

The repository of the Center for Disease Control's data.

The National Center on Addiction and Substance Abuse

http://www.casacolumbia.org/

The Web page of the thinktank devoted to providing resources on understanding the abuse of illegal substances.

National Organization for Women

http://now.org/now/home.html

A collection of onsite information and links to other Web sites for women's issues.

Nijenrode Business Webserver

http://www.nijenrode.nl/nbr/index.html

Searchable guide to online business resources, focused on the needs of students, faculty, and researchers.

On-Line Literary Resources

http://www.english.upenn.edu/~jlynch/Lit/

part
2

A searchable categorized directory of extensive academic sources of information in English and American literature.

Postmodern Culture

`http://jefferson.village.virginia.edu/pmc/contents.all.html`

Complete collection of the online journal of post-modernism.

Project Gutenberg

`http://www.promo.net/pg/`

The continuing project to make ASCII text versions of public domain classic literature available online; currently nearing 1,000 titles.

Religion

`http://sunfly.ub.uni-freiburg.de/religion/`

A starting point for studies in world religions.

Resources for Diversity

`http://www.nova.edu/Inter-Links/diversity.html`

A compilation of links to resources in issues of diversity.

Rhetoric and Composition

`http://english-server.hss.cmu.edu/rhetoric/`

An extensive guide to rhetoric, from the ancients to modern composition theory.

Suicide Information and Education Center (SIEC)

`http://www.siec.ca/`

Onsite resources, information, and links to more sites on issues of suicide prevention.

Thomas

http://Thomas.loc.gov/

A searchable database of all bills before the most recent sessions of the House of Representatives.

U.S. Civil War Center

http://www.cwc.lsu.edu/civlink.htm

An index of over 2,100 Civil War related Internet sites.

U.S. Senate

http://www.senate.gov/

A guide to business of the U.S. Senate.

United States Census Bureau Home Page

http://www.census.gov

A gold mine of statistics about the U.S. population.

University of Virginia Electronic Text Library

http://etext.lib.virginia.edu/uvaonline.html

Provides access to the University of Virginia's extensive collection of digitized texts and images.

Voice of the Shuttle: Web Page for Humanities Research

http://humanitas.ucsb.edu/

An amazingly comprehensive directory of humanities-oriented Web pages.

Welfare and Families

http://epn.org/idea/welfare.html

The Electronic Policy Network's electronic journal, archives, and links.

part

2

White House

http://www.whitehouse.gov/WH/Welcome.html

The starting point for Executive Branch information.

World Intellectual Property Organization (WIPO)

http://www.wipo.org/eng/index.htm

A guide to resources on copyrights and patents in the electronic age.

World Wide Arts Resources

http://wwar.world-arts-resources.com/

A searchable gateway to the arts online, plus a directory of Web sites, chats and bulletin boards.

part

2

 Current Events

CNN

http://www.cnn.com/

Multimedia, up-to-the minute online news source; not adequately archived for searches.

Electronic Newsstand

http://www.enews.com/

An extensive listing of thousands of magazines; searchable, though most articles founds are not available online.

Forbes

http://www.forbes.com/

Online version of *Forbes Magazine*; searchable archives.

Fox News

http://www.foxnews.com/

News, business, health, sports, and technology.

The New York Times on the Web

`http://www.nytimes.com/`

The New York Times on the Web. Requires registration, but free.

The New York Times on the Web: Books

`http://www.nytimes.com/books/`

Web-based book section of the *Times*.

Newsstand

`http://www.ecola.com/news/`

Links to over 4,200 Web site of print publications—newspapers, magazines, computer publications. Searchable by publication name.

San Francisco Chronicle

`http://www.sfgate.com/chronicle/`

Online version; searchable.

Time Magazine

`http://pathfinder.com/time/`

An online version of *Time Magazine*; search feature searches *Time* and many others; also provide access to bulletin boards and chats.

TotalNEWS

`http://totalnews.com/`

According to itself, "Information is the oxygen of the modern age. TotalNEWS is a directory of news sites designed to increase your access to information."

USA TODAY

`http://www.usatoday.com/`

Online version of the national newspaper.

part

2

Washington Post

http://www.washingtonpost.com/

Online version of the *Washington Post*; searchable for past week.

Bibliographic Citation Guides

American Psychological Association (APA) Guide to Style

http://www.wilpaterson.edu/wpcpages/library/apa.htm

Online version of the *APA Guide*; abridged.

Bibliographic Styles Handbook: APA

http://www.english.uiuc.edu/cws/wworkshop/apamenu.htm

A hypertext index to the APA publication style, from the University of Illinois at Urbana–Champaign.

Citing Electronic Materials with the New MLA Guidelines

http://www-dept.usm.edu/~engdept/mla/rules.html

Modified MLA guidelines to apply to electronic sources

Columbia Online Style

http://www.cas.usf.edu/english/walker/mla.html

The Alliance for Computers and Writing-endorsed guide to documenting online sources.

MLA Style

http://www.mla.org/main_stl.htm

The official site of MLA and its most current guide to publication style.

Modern Language Association (MLA) Guide to Style

http://www.wilpaterson.edu/wpcpages/library/mla.htm

Online version of the MLA Guide; abridged.

Finding Email Addresses

Bigfoot

http://www.bigfoot.com

Supposedly the Internet's largest collection of email addresses.

Four11

http://www.four11.com/

An extensive searchable email address directory, plus "yellow pages," a phone book, government and celebrity addresses.

Internet Address Finder

http://www.iaf.net/

Claims to be the fastest email search engine, with nearly six million addresses in its database.

Lycos EmailFind

http://www.lycos.com/emailfind.html

Associated with the Lycos Web search engine.

Phonebooke [sic]

http://www.phonebooke.com/

Searches Yahoo!, Usenet, and its own email address database.

Switchboard

http://www.switchboard.com/

One of the most popular "people-finders" on the Internet; good for addresses and phone numbers, thin on email addresses.

part

2

Usenet Addresses Database

`http://usenet-addresses.mit.edu/`

A list of the email addresses of posters to Usenet (actually a huge number, when you think about it).

WhoWhere

`http://www.whowhere.com/`

One of the first, and still one of the most used, people finders: email addresses, phone numbers, home pages, business and government Web and email addresses, 800 numbers, yellow pages, and more.

World Email Directory

`http://www.worldemail.com/`

Spreads itself thin, but your best chance at finding a non-U.S. address.

part

2

Documentation

 ## MLA Documentation of Electronic Sources

This section illustrates the new guidelines for electronic sources included in the recently published second edition of the *MLA Style Manual and Guide to Scholarly Publishing* (New York: MLA, 1998). For additional information about the MLA's new style manual, see *MLA on the Web* <http://www.mla.org/>, a site that is also useful for its list of frequently asked questions about MLA style.

Electronic texts appear in a variety of forms, and new ones appear with some frequency. Many electronic texts have print counterparts (e.g., newspaper and journal articles), and the examples that follow show how the MLA has adapted older forms to accommodate these new media. At times, it may be necessary to improvise in the same spirit. As in documenting any source, the most important function of the citation is to allow readers to locate that text for themselves. For that reason, keep the following guidelines in mind:

■ Use the whole uniform resource locator (URL), beginning with the mode of access (e.g., *http, FTP, Gopher*) and including all the extensions following the first single slash mark. Be sure to check this portion of the entry for accuracy. If you are able to move back and forth between the online source you are reading and a document you are creating, you might consider copying the URL and pasting it in the document to ensure accuracy.

■ Provide as much of the requested information as is available. It will often be necessary to look at several pages of a Web document to find such things as the organization sponsoring the Web page or the date of the latest version. When a piece of information is not available (and sometimes it is not), then go on to the next item.

■ Give the date of access as well as the date of publication given in the document. Because electronic texts can be revised easily and revision dates are not always given, there is no guarantee that the text a writer cites will be the one a reader retrieves. The date of access helps to account for any differences that may occur.

■ If it is necessary to divide a URL between lines in your works cited entry, divide it only after a slash mark. Neither a hyphen nor any other character should be used to indicate the division.

part

2

Note: Dividing the URL only after a slash may result in some odd-looking citations. The date of access and URL should begin on the same line and are not separated by any punctuation. In some cases, a URL divided at the slash mark may begin on the next line instead; in other cases, the line lengths will be noticeably uneven.

This guide is organized like the new *MLA Style Manual* by grouping electronic resources into five large categories: online scholarly projects, reference databases, and personal or professional sites; online books; articles in online periodicals; CD-ROMs; and other electronic sources (e.g., advertising, email). It also suggests formats for commercial online services (such as CompuServe, Dialog, or America Online) that are not clearly covered by the new style manual.

An Online Scholarly Project, Reference Database, or Professional or Personal Site

An entry for an entire online scholarly project or database should contain the following elements:

1. Title of the project or database (underlined)

2. Name of the editor or director of the project or database (if given)

3. Electronic publication information, including version number, date of electronic publication or latest update, and name of sponsoring institution or organization

4. Date of access and electronic address (the latter in angle brackets)

The first group of examples illustrates how to cite an entire online scholarly project or reference database.

American Verse Project. 16 Oct. 1996. University of
     Michigan and Humanities Text Initiative. 15 June
     1998 <http://www.hti.umich.edu/english/amverse/>.

Microsoft Encarta Concise Encyclopedia. 1998.
     Microsoft. 15 June 1998 <http://encarta.msn.com/
     find/find.asp>.

Paul Laurence Dunbar Digital Text Archives. 1992.
     Wright State U. 15 June 1998 <http://
     www.libraries.wright.edu/dunbar/>.

The Perseus Project. Ed. Gregory R. Crane. Mar.
     1997. Dept. of Classics, Tufts U. 15 June 1998
     <http://www.perseus.tufts.edu/>.

Project Gutenberg. Ed. Michael S. Hart. 1998.
     Illinois Benedictine College. 15 June 1998
     <http://www.promo.net/pg/>.

It is much more common to use only a portion of a scholarly project or database. To cite an essay, poem, or other short work, begin with the author's name, followed by the title of the work within quotation marks, and the full information for the project. If the URL for the short work differs from that of the project, use the URL of the short work. As the following illustrations show, the difference can be considerable.

Martin, Thomas. "Overview of Archaic and Classical
     Greek History." The Perseus Project. Ed. Gregory
     R. Crane. Mar. 1997. Dept. of Classics, Tufts U.
     15 June 1998 <http://hydra.perseus.tufts.edu/
     cgi-bin/text?lookup=trm+ov+toc>.

Wilde, Oscar. "Helas!" Project Gutenberg. Ed. Michael
     S. Hart. Oct. 1997. Illinois Benedictine College.

part

2

15 June 1998 <ftp://uiarchive.cso.uiuc.edu/pub/
etext/gutenberg/etext97/pmwld10.txt>.

To cite an anonymous article within a reference database, begin with
the name of the article (in quotation marks) and then provide the rest of
the information for the database. If the URL for the article differs from
that of the whole database, use the URL of the article, as in the following illustrations.

"Loch Ness Monster." <u>Encyclopedia Smithsonian</u>. 1994.
   Smithsonian Institution. 15 June 1998 <http://
   www.si.edu/resource/faq/nmnh/lochness.htm>.

"Nike." <u>The Perseus Project</u>. Ed. Gregory R. Crane.
   Mar. 1997. Dept. of Classics, Tufts U. 15 June
   1998 <http://www.perseus.tufts.edu/cgi-bin/
   lookup?lookup=nike>.

In addition to scholarly projects and reference databases, the new
MLA Style Manual identifies two other types of Web sites, professional
and personal. The *MLA on the Web* entry below demonstrates the first
category, and the home page of Paul Brians illustrates the second. Also
included are some web sites that do not fit clearly into either category.
The Margaret Atwood Information Web Site combines the two categories; although it is the Canadian author's own Web site, it is maintained on her behalf by a number of other people. Still other Web sites
might be thought of as "commercial" sites, since they are maintained by
companies but are really not advertisements in the usual sense. The illustration drawn from the the Levi Strauss Web site demonstrates how such
information might be documented.

part

2

Atwood, Margaret. <u>The Margaret Atwood Information
   Web Site</u>. 15 June 1998 <http://www.web.net/
   owtoad/frame.htm>.

<u>The Atwood Society's Margaret Atwood Information
   Site</u>. 19 May 1998. The Margaret Atwood Society
   and Thomas B. Friedman. 15 June 1998 <http://
   www.cariboo.bc.ca/atwood/>.

Brians, Paul. Home page. 16 June 1997 <http://
   www.wsu.edu:8080/~brians/index.html>.

"The History of Levi's 501 Jeans." <u>Levi Strauss.com</u>.
1997. 18 June 1998 <http://www.levistrauss.com/
lsc_history_501.html>.

<u>MLA on the Web</u>. 1997. 15 June 1998 <http://
www.mla.org/>.

An Online Book

Online books may be part of a scholarly project or published independently. The citation for an independently published book should contain the following items:

1. Author's name. If only an editor, compiler, or translator is identified, cite that name, followed by the appropriate abbreviation (*ed.*, *comp.*, *trans.*)

2. Title of the work (underlined)

3. Name of the editor, compiler, or translator

4. Publication information. If the online version has not been published before, give the date of electronic publication and name of any sponsoring institution or organization. State the publication facts about the original print version if they are given; you may use square brackets to add relevant information not provided in the source.

5. Date of access and electronic address (the latter in angle brackets)

Dickens, Charles. <u>The Cricket on the Hearth</u>. [1846].
16 June 1998 <ftp://ftp.books.com/ebooks/Fiction/
Authors/D/Dickens/CRICKET.TXT>.

Stork, David G., ed. <u>Hal's Legacy: 2001's Computer
as Dream and Reality</u>. Cambridge: MIT P, 1996. 16
June 1998 <http://mitpress.mit.edu/e-books/Hal/>.

Turgenev, Ivan. <u>Fathers and Sons</u> . 1861. Trans.
Richard Hare. [London]: Hutchinson, 1948.
16 June 1998 <http://eldred.ne.mediaone.net/ist/
fas.htm>.

To cite a book that is part of a scholarly project, provide the relevant information from the five items outlined above, followed by publication information for the project. If the URL of the book and the project differ, use the URL of the book.

Austen, Jane. <u>Emma</u>. <u>Project Gutenberg</u>. Ed. Michael
    S. Hart. Aug. 1994. Illinois Benedictine College.
    15 June 1998 <ftp://uiarchive.cso.uiuc.edu/pub/
    etext/gutenberg/etext94/emma10.txt>.

Dunbar, Paul Laurence. <u>Lyrics of Lowly Life</u>. New
    York: Dodd, 1896. <u>Paul Laurence Dunbar Digital</u>
    <u>Text Archives</u>. 1992. Wright State U. 15 June
    1998 <http://www.library.wright.edu/dunbar/
    lowly1.html#Contents17>.

To cite part of an online book, place the title or name or the part between the author's name and the title of the book. Punctuate the title of the part of the book as you would if it were in print (e.g., the title of an essay or poem would be in quotation marks, but a preface or introduction would have no special punctuation). If the URLs of the book and the portion you are citing differ, include the URL of the part you are using. The two illustrations are different portions of the same online book.

Dunbar, Paul Laurence. "An Ante-Bellum Sermon."
    <u>Lyrics of Lowly Life</u>. New York: Dodd, 1896.
    <u>Paul Laurence Dunbar Digital Text Archives</u>.
    1992. Wright State U. 15 June 1998 <http://
    www.libraries.wright.edu/dunbar/
    lowly2.html#lowly18>.

Howells, William Dean. Introduction. <u>Lyrics of</u>
    <u>Lowly Life</u>. By Paul Laurence Dunbar. New York:
    Dodd, 1896. <u>Paul Laurence Dunbar Digital Text</u>
    <u>Archives</u>. 1992. Wright State U. 15 June 1998
    <http://www.library.wright.edu/dunbar/
    lowly1.html#Contents58>.

part

2

An Article in an Online Periodical

Online periodicals fit into much the same categories as their print counterparts—scholarly journals, newspapers, magazines—and the forms for citing them are similar. The citation should contain the following elements:

1. Author's name

2. Title of the work or material (quotation marks) (If a review or letter to the editor is unnamed, use the appropriate descriptive term—e.g., *letter*—without quotation marks.)

3. Name of the periodical (underlined)

4. Volume number, issue number, or other identifying number

5. Date of publication

6. The number range or total number of pages, paragraphs, or other sections, if numbered

7. Date of access and electronic address (the latter in angle brackets)

a. An Article in a Scholarly Journal

Best, Michael. "From Book to Screen: A Window on Renaissance Electronic Texts." <u>Early Modern Literary Studies</u> 1.2 (1995): 27 pars. 17 June 1998 <http://purl.oclc.org/emls/01-2/bestbook.html>.

Chiel, Hillel J. "Critical Thinking in a Neuro-biology Course." <u>Bioscene</u> 22 (1996): 13 pp. 17 June 1998 <http://papa.indstate.edu/amcbt/volume_22/v22n1s3.html>.

George, Pamela G. "The Effectiveness of Cooperative Learning Strategies in Multicultural University Classrooms." <u>Journal on Excellence in College Teaching</u> 5.1 (1994): 21-30. 16 June 1998 <http://www.lib.muohio.edu/ject/html/v5n1/v5n1-George.html>.

Hubona, Geoffrey S., Gregory W. Shirah, and David G. Fout. "The Effect of Motion and Stereopsis on Three-Dimensional Visualization." <u>International Journal of Human-Computer Studies</u> 4 (1997): 609-27. 16 June 1998 <http://fai.idealibrary.com:80/cgi-bin/fai.idealibrary.com_8100/class;CFmedia::CMDApplication;deliver/0100015f040402000f060d02015f01060508/130:1121:58319/article.pdf>.

part **2**

b. An Article in a Newspaper or on a Newswire

"Au Pair's Hometown Cheers Ruling." <u>AP Online</u> 16
    June 1998. 16 June 1998 <http://www.nytimes.com/
    aponline/I/AP-Britain-Au-Pair-Reaction.html>.

Griffiths, Paul. "Looking for Love in Bizet's
    Highland Fling." <u>New York Times</u> 29 June 1998.
    Electronic. America Online. 29 June 1998.

King, Sharon R. "Monday's Stocks: U.S. Stocks
    Plunge as Asian Turmoil Worsens." <u>New York
    Times on the Web</u> 16 June 1998. 16 June 1998
    <http://www.nytimes.com/yr/mo/day/news/financial/
    market.html>.

(**Note:** The Griffiths article was obtained through a commercial online
service that does not use a URL. See pages 106–107 for a more detailed
explanation about documenting such sources.)

c. An Article in a Magazine

Caldwell, Christopher. "The Southern Captivity of
    the GOP." <u>Atlantic Monthly</u> June 1998: 55–72. 16
    June 1998 <http://www.theatlantic.com/issues/
    current/gop.htm>.

Jellinek, George. "Bryn Terfel Sings Heroic Handel
    Arias." <u>Stereo Review</u> Apr. 1998. Electronic.
    America Online. 29 June 1998.

Johnson, Roy S. "The Jordan Effect." <u>Fortune</u> 22 June
    1998. 16 June 1998 <http://www.pathfinder.com/
    fortune/1998/980622/jor.html>.

Stone, Peter S. "The Nicotine Network." <u>Mother
    Jones</u> May-June 1996. 16 June 1998 <http://
    www.mojones.com/mother_jones/MJ96/stone2.html>.

(**Notes:** The Jellinek article was obtained through a commercial online
service that does not use a URL. See pages 106–107 for a more detailed
explanation about documenting such sources. The dates in the third
illustration above really are correct. The story about Michael Jordan
was available online several days earlier than the publication date that
appears on the cover of the magazine.)

d. A Review

Rodger, Blake. Rev. of <u>Milton's Imperial Epic:</u>
<u>Paradise Lost and the Discourse of Colonialism</u>,
by Martin Evans. <u>Milton Review</u> 13 (1998). 16 June
1998. <http://www.richmond.edu/~creamer/
mr13.html>.

Schickel, Richard. "Childhood Mightmares." Rev. of
<u>The Butcher Boy,</u> dir. Neil Jordan. <u>Time</u> 6 Apr.
1998. 17 June 1998 <http://www.pathfinder.com/
time/magazine/1998/dom/980406/
the_arts.cinema.childhoo18.html>.

e. An Abstract

Hubona, Geoffrey S., Gregory W. Shirah, and David G.
Fout. "The Effect of Motion and Stereopsis on
Three-Dimensional Visualization." <u>International</u>
<u>Journal of Human-Computer Studies</u> 4 (1997):
609–27. Abstract. 16 June 1998
<http://fai.idealibrary.com:80/
cgi-bin/fai.idealibrary.com_8100/fetch/
0100015f040402020f070701035703050f03/
130:1123:4203/0>.

f. An Editorial

"Michael's Last Hurrah?" Editorial. <u>New York Times</u>
<u>on the Web</u> 16 June 1998. 15 June 1998 <http://
www.nytimes.com/yr/mo/day/editorial/16tue3.html>.

Smith, Harriet. Editorial. <u>International Piano</u>
<u>Quarterly</u> Winter 1998. 15 June 1998 <http://
www.gramophone.co.uk/i.html>.

g. A Letter to the Editor

Montague, Paul. Letter. <u>Time</u> 23 Mar. 1998. 17 June
1998 <http://www.pathfinder.com/time/magazine/
1998/dom/980323/letters.letters.28.html>.

part
2

Publications on CD-ROM, Diskette, or Magnetic Tape

Many texts appear in several formats, such as print, CD-ROM, diskette, or magnetic tape. The forms for electronic versions of these sources are similar to their print counterparts. The MLA divides these sources into two categories—nonperiodical publications and periodical publications. The first kind is published as a book would be; that is, published once, without any plan for updates. The second kind is published on a regular schedule, like a journal or magazine.

The entry for a nonperiodical publication on CD-ROM, diskettte or magnetic tape consists of the following items:

1. Author's name (if given). If the name of an editor, compiler, or translator is given instead, cite that person's name, followed by the appropriate abbreviation (*ed., comp., trans.*)

2. Title of the publication (underlined)

3. Name of editor, compiler, or translator (if relevant)

4. Publication medium (*CD-ROM, Diskette,* or *Magnetic tape*)

5. Edition, release, or version (if relevant), using the appropriate abbreviation (*Ed., Rel., Vers.*)

6. Place of publication

7. Name of publisher

8. Date of publication

The date of access is not included because these media cannot be revised in the same way that online publications can. The first examples below demonstrate how to cite an entire work on CD-ROM. An entry for a diskette or magnetic tape would be done in the same way, with only the medium changed. If some of the information in not provided, cite whatever is available. (In the second illustration, neither the CD-ROM nor the material accompanying it is dated.)

Ingpen, Robert, and Philip Wilkinson. <u>Ideas That Changed the World</u>. CD-ROM. Toronto: ICE Integrated Communications and Entertainment, 1996.

<u>World's Greatest Speeches</u>. CD-ROM. Irvine: Softbit, n.d.

part

2

If publication information for a printed version is provided, begin the citation with that information.

Coleridge, Samuel Taylor. <u>The Complete Works of Samuel Taylor Coleridge</u>. Ed. Ernest Hartley Coleridge. 2 vols. Oxford: Clarendon, 1912. <u>English Poetry Full-Text Database</u>. Rel. 2. CD-ROM. Cambridge, Engl: Chadwyck, 1993.

If you are citing only part of a work, identify the part and punctuate the title appropriately (e.g., underline the title of a book-length work or use quotation marks for an article, poem, or short story). If the source provides numbers for pages, paragraphs, screens, or some other division, include that information.

Bryan, William Jennings. "The Cross of Gold." <u>World's Greatest Speeches</u>. CD-ROM. Irvine: Softbit, n.d.

Coleridge, Samuel Taylor. "An Ode to the Rain." <u>The Complete Works of Samuel Taylor Coleridge</u>. Ed. Ernest Hartley Coleridge. Vol. 1. Oxford: Clarendon, 1912. 382–84. <u>English Poetry Full-Text Database</u>. Rel. 2. CD-ROM. Cambridge, Engl: Chadwyck, 1993.

Ingpen, Robert, and Philip Wilkinson. "Babbage's Machines." <u>Ideas That Changed the World</u>. CD-ROM. Toronto: ICE Integrated Communictions and Entertainment, 1996.

The form for citing CD-ROMs that are published periodically is similar to that for nonperiodical publications. It contains the following items:

1. Author's name (if given)

2. Publication information for any identified printed source or analogue

3. Title of the database (underlined)

4. Publication medium

5. Name of the vendor (if relevant). (Some information providers lease their data to vendors, such as SilverPlatter or UMI-Proquest, rather than publishing it themselves.)

6. Electronic publication date

Once again, the date of access is not required. The first example below illustrates how to document a portion of a work published periodically in one of these media. The second illustrates how to document the whole work.

Trail, George Y. "Teaching Argument and the
    Rhetoric of Orwell's 'Politics and the English
    Language.' " <u>College English</u> 57 (1995): 570–83.
    Abstract. <u>ERIC</u>. CD-ROM. SilverPlatter. Sept.
    1996.

United States. Dept. of Commerce. Bureau of the
    Census. <u>U.S. Imports of Merchandise</u>. CD-ROM. Data
    User Services Division. Mar. 1994.

Other Electronic Sources

In addition to the electronic sources described above, MLA provides guidelines for a number of other media.

a. A Television or Radio Program

Caplan, Jeff. "The Best Way to Put Out a Hit on
    Mosquitos." <u>Healthy Living</u>. CBS Radio. WCBS,
    New York. 16 June 1998. Transcript. 17 June 1998
    <http://www.newsradio88.com/health/history/
    june_1998/june_16.html>.

b. A Sound Recording or Sound Clip

Schumann, Robert. "Arabesque." <u>The Romantic Piano</u>.
    WCLV, 1997. 17 June 1998 <http://www.wclv.com/
    sounds/arabesk.mp2>.

c. A Film or Film Clip

Softley, Iain, dir. <u>The Wings of the Dove</u>. Miramax,
    1997. 18 June 1998 <http://www.hollywood.com/
    trailers/wingsdove/high_wingsdove.ram>.

part

2

d. A Work of Art

Simmons, John. <u>Titania</u>. 1866. Bristol Museums
    and Art Gallery. 17 June 1998 <http://
    www.nextcity.com/go/ago/>.

van Gogh, Vincent. <u>The Starry Night</u>. 1889. Museum
    of Modern Art, New York. 16 June 1998 <http://
    www.moma.org/collection/paintsculpt/
    vangogh.starry.html>.

e. An Interview

Atwood, Margaret. Interview with Marilyn Snell.
    <u>Mother Jones</u> July-Aug. 1997. 18 June 1998
    <http://www.motherjones.com/mother_jones/JA97/
    visions.html>.

f. A Map

"Hobart, Oklahoma." Map. <u>U.S. Gazetteer</u>. US Census
    Bureau. 17 June 1998 <http://www.census.gov/
    cgi-bin/gazetteer?city=Hobart&state=OK&zip=>.

g. A Cartoon

Stossel, Sage. "Even Better Than Viagra." Cartoon.
    <u>Atlantic Monthly</u> 20 May 1998. 29 June 1998
    <http://www2.theAtlantic.com/atlantic/unbound/
    sage/ss980520.htm>.

h. An Advertisement

Toyota Land Cruiser. Advertisement. 17 June
    1998 <http://www.toyota.com/
    welcome@SK@0rY0Z11f27T1C@@.html>.

i. A Manuscript or Working Paper

Davis, George K., and Bryce E. Kanago. "The
    Correlation Between Prices and Output:
    Controlling for Contaminating Dynamics." Working
    paper, n.d. <http://www.sba.muohio.edu/davisgk/
    Research/pycor.pdf>.

part

2

Whitman, Walt. "Live Oak, with Moss." Ms. Valentine-
    Barrett Collection. University of Virginia. 17
    June 1998 <http://jefferson.village.virginia.edu/
    whitman/manuscripts/moss/oak1.html>.

j. An Email Communication To cite email sent to an individual, give the name of the writer, the title of the message (the subject line) in quotation marks, a description that includes the name of the recipient, and the date the message was sent. In the first example, the word *author* refers to the person writing the paper in which the email message is being cited.

Smith, Ray. "Re: Pride and Prejudice Adaptations."
    Email to the author. 1 July 1998.

Willis, Jonathan. Email to Margaret Taylor. 28 June
    1998.

k. An Online Posting Citing email posted to a discussion list calls for more detailed information. It should provide the name of the author, the title of the message (the subject lines) in quotation marks, a description (*Online posting*), the date the message was posted, the name of the discussion list, the date of access, and the Internet site or email address of the list in angle brackets. The form will be the same whether you are citing an email list (the Williams example), a World Wide Web forum (Roth), or a Usenet news group (Lamming). Whenever possible, cite an archived copy of the message, which is easier for readers to retrieve. The Curtis example below is an archival version rather than the initial posting.

Curtis, Richard. "Group Dynamnics Training for
    Leaders." Online posting. 12 Nov. 1993. Wildornt
    Discussion Group. 1 July 1998 <gopher://
    lists.Princeton.EDU:70/0R8935-9654-/wildornt/
    logs/log9311>.

Lamming, Andrew. "Faroe-ese??" Online posting.
    23 June 1998. 29 June 1998
    <news:comp.edu.languages.natural>.

Roth, Kevin. Online posting. 30 Oct. 1997. Athletes
    Behaving Badly. 29 June 1998 <http://
    forums.nytimes.com/webin/WebX?13@^9878@.ee9a6af/0>.

part

2

Williams, Angela. "Re: Tutor Certification." Online
    posting. 16 June 1998. WAC-L. 18 June 1998
    <wac-l@postoffice.cso.uiuc.edu>.

If you want to cite a document that has been forwarded as part of
another posting, begin with the name of the writer, the title, and the date
of the original document. Continue with the name of the person who
forwarded that posting and then provide the appropriate information for
the posting in which the document was forwarded. The illustration
below refers to Richard Curtis's original message (illustrated above) that
was forwarded in Sandy Kohn's message.

Curtis, Richard. "Group Dynamnics Training for
    Leaders." 12 Nov. 1993. Fwd. by Sandy Kohn.
    Online posting. 15 Nov. 1993. Wildornt
    Discussion Group. 1 July 1998 <gopher://
    lists.Princeton.EDU:70/0R9654-10956-/wildornt/
    logs/log9311>.

part

2

I. A Synchronous Communication To cite a communication that
took place in a MUD (multiuser domain) or MOO (multiuser domain,
object-oriented), give the name of the speaker (if you cite only one), a
description of the event, the date of the event, the forum for the event
(MiamiMoo and LinguaMOO in the examples below), and the address.
If you cite more than one speaker, begin with the description of the
event. If the event has been archived, cite that version so that readers
can consult it. The first example below illustrates an archived version
of a single paper presented at an online conference that took place on a
MOO; the second illustrates how to cite the entire conference. The final
illustration demonstrates how to cite an individual exchange that took
place on a MOO.

Haynes-Burton, Cynthia. Online conference presenta-
    tion. "Writing and Community: The Use of MOOs in
    the Teaching of Writing." "Text-Based Virtual
    Reality: What Is It and How Is It Being Used?"
    Online conference. 11 Oct. 1994. LinguaMOO. 18
    June 1998 <http://www.utdallas.edu/~cynthiah/
    lingua_archive/meridian-moo-seminar.txt>.

"Text-Based Virtual Reality: What Is It and How Is
    It Being Used?" Online conference. 11 Oct. 1994.

LinguaMOO. 18 June 1998 <http://www.utdallas.edu/
~cynthiah/lingua_archive/meridian-moo-
seminar.txt>.

Wallrodt, Susan. Online discussion of virtual Delphi
site. 18 June 1998. MiamiMoo. 18 June 1998
<telnet://moo.cas.muohio.edu>.

Sources from a Commercial Online Service

The new *MLA Style Manual* says nothing about how to cite materials
provided by a commercial service, such as CompuServe or America Online. In many cases, there is no need for a special citation form. For example, anyone using one of these services to access sites on the World
Wide Web will have the URL and other necessary information at hand
and can simply follow the MLA format for Web sites. However, some
sources of information are available only to those who subscribe to that
service. Until the MLA develops a specific form for citing commercial
services, the best course is probably to supply the information that
would be needed for a reader to locate that source. The following examples demonstrate how to document such sources in ways consistent with
MLA style. Like the other forms, these begin with the name of the author, the title of the work, and the date it was posted or updated. The
word *Electronic* is used to identify the medium, the name of the service
follows, and the citation ends with the date of access.

part

2

Dunbar, William. "Lament for the Makaris Quhen He
Was Sek." Representative Poetry On-Line. U of
Toronto P, 1996. Rep. Poetry 2RP1.55. Electronic.
America Online. 24 June 1998.

"Censorship." <u>Merriam Webster Dictionary</u>. 1998 ed.
Electronic. America Online. 30 June 1998.

Griffiths, Paul. "Looking for Love in Bizet's
Highland Fling." <u>New York Times</u> 29 June 1998.
Electronic. America Online. 29 June 1998.

Jellinek, George. "Bryn Terfel Sings Heroic Handel
Arias." <u>Stereo Review</u> Apr. 1998. Electronic.
America Online. 29 June 1998.

"Run with It." Bob's Fitness Tips. Oprah Online.
29 Jan. 1998. Electronic. America Online. 24 June
1998.

Citing Electronic Sources in the Text

In principle, electronic sources are cited the same way as print sources in the body of a paper. For citing an entire work, only the name of the author (or the title, if no author is identified) is required. Quoting, paraphrasing, or otherwise referring to a specific passage in a printed source calls for the author's name (or the title, if no author is identified) and a page number. If an electronic source contains page, paragraph, or screen numbers, they can be used. With page numbers, use only the author's name and the page number, as when citing a print source; use the author's name, followed by a comma, and the abbreviation *par.* or the word *screen* in addition to the number. If there are no numbers, use only the author's name (or the title, if no author is idenfitied). The following illustrations are drawn from the examples used earlier.

Citing an Entire Work

Although Michael Jordan's economic impact on basketball has been enormous, it cannot be measured in simple terms (Johnson).

or

As Roy S. Johnson points out, Michael Jordan's economic impact on basketball has been enormous, but it cannot be measured in simple terms.

Citing Part of a Work

Document with page numbers

George Davis and Bryce Kanago suggest that recessions can be generated by large supply shocks, large demand shocks, or a combination of both (12).

or

Economists at Miami University suggest that recessions can be generated by large supply shocks, large demand shocks, or a combination of both (Davis and Kanago 12).

Document with numbered paragraphs

Michael Best warns that trying to make online books seem like printed books may lead to seeing the screen simply as "a poor imitation of the original book" (par. 1).

or

The effort to make online books seem like printed books may lead to seeing the screen simply as "a poor imitation of the original book" (Best, par. 1).

Document without page, paragraph, or screen numbers

Paul Montague is skeptical of the agreement reached between U.N. Secretary-General Kofi Annan and Saddam Hussein, reminding readers of British Prime Minister Neville Chamberlain's 1938 meeting with Hitler and the 1939 invasion of Poland.

or

One commentator is skeptical of the agreement reached between U.N. Secretary-General Kofi Annan and Saddam Hussein, reminding readers of British Prime Minister Neville Chamberlain's 1938 meeting with Hitler and the 1939 invasion of Poland (Montague).

Document with no author identified

On May 20, 1873, Levi Strauss and Jacob Davis were granted a patent for their riveted pants, which they called "waist overalls" ("History").

or

According to "The History of Levi's 501 Jeans," the patent for riveted pants, called "waist overalls," was granted to Levi Strauss and Jacob Davis on May 20, 1873.

part

2

APA Documentation of Electronic Sources

The electronic documentation formats found in the fourth edition of the *Publication Manual of the American Psychological Association* are based on X. Li and N. B. Crane's *Electronic Style: A Guide to Citing Electronic Information* (Westport, CT: Meckler, 1993). The APA has updated some of its formats for material with a print equivalent at a Web site: http://www.apa.org/journals/webref.html. Li and Crane have continued to update their book on the following Web site: http://www.uvm.edu/~ncrane/estyles/apa.html. The formats discussed in this section are based on both available APA models and models provided by Li and Crane at their Web site.

When citing electronic media, you should use the standard APA format to identify authorship, date of origin (if known), and title, much as you would for print material; then add a clear indication of the path or address for the electronic source. In case your instructor has a distinct preference as to how you list source data from online computer networks, you should confirm the details of electronic citation forms before finalizing any copy.

To comply with APA style, present information in the following general sequence when citing online sources:

- The author's or editor's last name and initials
- The year of the work in parentheses (write *no date* if the electronic publication date is not available)
- The title of the complete work, underlined or italicized
- The type of electronic medium in brackets, for example, [Online]
- The producer of the database or Web site (optional)
- The designation *Available:*, followed by the access protocol, path or URL
- The date of access or visit in the order year, month, day, in brackets

1. An online professional or personal site.

Jarvis, P. (No date). <u>My Homepage.</u> [Online].
    Available: http://www.mtu.edu/~students [1997,
    December 3].

<u>Victoriana—Resources for Victorian Living.</u>
  (1996-1997). [Online]. Reflections of the Past—
  Antiques. Available: http://www.victoriana.com
  [1998, January 20].

2. An online book. For an online book, provide any data on the print publication before details on where the electronic version may be located.

Aristotle. (1954). <u>Rhetoric.</u> W. R. Roberts, Trans.
  [Online] The English Server at Carnegie Mellon
  University. Available: http://www.rpi.edu/
  ~honeyl/Rhetoric/index.html [1997, April 8].

3. An article in an online work. Generally, citations for articles in online works follow the same sequence as citations for their print counterparts.

Women in American History. (1998). In <u>Encyclopedia
  Britannica</u> [Online]. Available: http://
  www.women.eb.com [1998, May 25].

An article in an online newspaper or on a newswire

Wright, R. (1998, February 4). U.S. wins support
  but no mandate against Iraq. <u>The Los Angeles
  Times</u> [Online], p. 1A. Available: http://
  www.latimes.com [1998, February 4].

Schmitt, E. (1998, February 4). Cohen promises
  "significant" military campaign against Iraq
  if diplomacy fails. <u>The New York Times on the
  Web</u> [Online], 6 paragraphs. Available: http://
  www.nytimes.com [1998, February 4].

An article in an online magazine

Thakker, S. (1998, May). Avoiding automobile theft.
  <u>Ontario Police Crime Prevention Magazine</u> [Online],
  3 paragraphs. Available: http://www.opcpm.com/
  inside/avoidingautomobile.html [1998, May 26].

part

2

An online review

Spiers, S. (1998). [Review of the report on blood
poisoning by <u>Prevention/NBCToday</u>]. <u>OBGYN.net</u>
[Online], 10 paragraphs. Available: http://
www.obgyn.net/women/archives [1998, August 3].

An online editorial

Spilner, M. (1998, May). Walking club welcome.
<u>Prevention</u> [Online], 5 paragraphs. Available:
http://www.nytimes.com//yr/mo/day/letters [1998,
May 6].

An online letter to the editor

Rivel, D. (1998, May 6). Art in the schools. <u>The
New York Times on the Web</u> [Online letter to
the editor], 4 paragraphs. Available: http://
www.nytimes.com//yr/mo/day/letters [1998, May 6].

An article in an online scholarly journal

Britt, R. (1995). The heat is on: Scientists
agree on human contribution to global warming.
<u>Ion Science</u> [Online]. Available: http://
www.injersey.com/Media/IonSci/features/gwarm
[1996, November 13].

4. A nonperiodical publication on CD-ROM, magnetic tape or diskette. To
cite works distributed on CDs, disks, or magnetic tape, give the author(s),
publication date, title, and publication information in standard APA format. After the title, identify the type of electronic medium in brackets,
for example, [CD-ROM].

Reid, Joy. (1983). Computer-assisted text-analysis
for ESL students [CD-ROM]. <u>Calico Journal,</u> 1, 3,
40-42. Abstract from: Dialog File: Eric Item:
EJ298270

5. An online work of art.

Seurat, G. (1884). <u>A Sunday Afternoon on the Island
of La Grand Jatte</u> [Online]. Art Institute of
Chicago. Available: http://www.artic.edu/aic/
collections [1998, Aug. 3].

6. An online interview.

Jorgenson, L. (1998, May 26). For a change, Jazz
feel bullish: Interview with Jeff Hornacek.
<u>Deseret News</u> [Online], 15 paragraphs. Available:
http://www.desnews.com/playoffs [1998, May 26].

7. An online posting. Although email is not included in APA References, somewhat more public or accessible Internet postings from newsgroups or listservs may be included if they are retrievable in some form.

Shaumann, T. (1994, August 5). Technical German.
<u>Technical German Discussion List</u> [Online].
Available: Email:
usenet@comp.edu.languages.natural [1994,
September 7].

Heilke, J. (1996, May 3). Webfolios. <u>Alliance for
Computers and Writing Discussion List</u> [Online].
Available: ttu.edu/lists/acw-1/9605 [1996,
December 31].

8. An online synchronous communication.

Worldmoo Computer Club. (1998, February 3).
Available: telnet:world.sensemedia.net1234 [1998,
February 3].

part

2

Glossary

Your Own Private Glossary

The Glossary in this book contains reference terms you'll find useful as you get started on the Internet. After a while, however, you'll find yourself running across abbreviations, acronyms, and buzzwords whose definitions will make more sense to you once you're no longer a novice (or "newbie"). That's the time to build a glossary of your own. For now, the 2DNet Webopædia gives you a place to start.

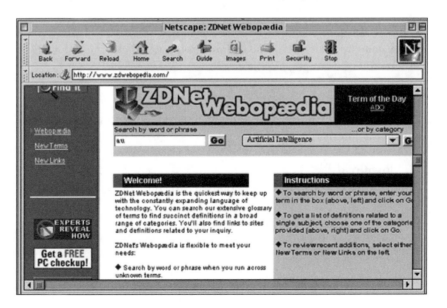

alias
A simple email address that can be used in place of a more complex one.

bandwidth
Internet parlance for capacity to carry or transfer information such as email and Web pages.

browser
The computer program that lets you view the contents of Web sites.

client
A program that runs on your personal computer and supplies you with Internet services, such as getting your mail.

DNS
See **domain name server.**

domain
A group of computers administered as a single unit, typically belonging to a single organization such as a university or corporation.

domain name
A name that identifies one or more computers belonging to a single domain. For example, "apple.com".

domain name server
A computer that converts domain names into the numeric addresses used on the Internet.

download
Copying a file from another computer to your computer over the Internet.

email
Electronic mail.

emoticon
A guide to the writer's feelings, represented by typed characters, such as the Smiley :-). Helps readers understand the emotions underlying a written message.

FAQ
Frequently Asked Questions

flame
A rude or derogatory message directed as a personal attack against an individual or group.

flame war
An exchange of flames (see above).

FTP
File Transfer Protocol, a method of moving files from one computer to another over the Internet.

home page
A page on the World Wide Web that acts as a starting point for information about a person or organization.

hypertext
Text that contains embedded *links* to other pages of text. Hypertext enables the reader to navigate between pages of related information by following links in the text.

link
A reference to a location on the Web that is embedded in the text of the Web page. Links are usually highlighted with a different color or underline to make them easily visible.

list server
Strictly speaking, a computer program that administers electronic mailing lists, but also used to denote such lists or discussion groups, as in "the writer's list server."

lurker
A passive reader of an Internet *newsgroup*. A lurker reads messages, but does not participate in the discussion by posting or responding to messages.

modem
A device for connecting two computers over a telephone line.

newbie
A new user of the Internet.

newsgroup
A discussion forum in which all participants can read all messages and public replies between the participants.

pages
All the text, graphics, pictures, and so forth, denoted by a single URL beginning with the identifier "http://".

quoted
Text in an email message or newsgroup posting that has been set off by the use of vertical bars or > characters in the left-hand margin.

search engine
A computer program that will locate Web sites or files based on specified criteria.

secure
A Web page whose contents are encrypted when sending or receiving information.

server
A computer program that moves information on request, such as a Web server that sends pages to your browser.

Smiley
See **emoticon**.

snail mail
Mail sent the old fashioned way: Write a letter, put it in an envelope, stick on a stamp, and drop it in the mailbox.

spam
Spam is to the Internet as unsolicited junk mail is to the postal system.

URL
Uniform Resource Locator: The notation for specifying addresses on the World Wide Web (e.g. http://www.abacon.com or ftp://ftp.abacon.com).

Usenet
The section of the Internet devoted to *newsgroups*.

Web site
A collection of pages administered by a single organization or individual.